Praise for
People without History Are Dust

"This book is excellent both with respect to Anna Hájková's deep immersion in the historiography and theoretical literature pertaining to the topic, but also with regards to her remarkable research of finding traces of people and the lives they lived that have remained invisible and inaudible in the history of the Holocaust."

Alexandra Garbarini, Hans W. Gatzke '38 Professor of Modern European History, Williams College

"Anna Hájková's pioneering work brings the stories of queer Holocaust victims to the fore, unearthing the bonds of kinship that sustained them in a time of genocide. This book is a passionate reminder of the power of queer desire in the midst of fascist violence."

Samuel Clowes Huneke, Associate Professor of History, George Mason University

"Anna Hájková's *People without History Are Dust* is at once an act of recovery – rescuing from obscurity and reframing stories of Holocaust-era same-sex desire and intimacy that had fallen through the cracks – and a courageous and powerful historiographic meditation. Hájková urges us not only to create more inclusive Holocaust narratives but also to queer Holocaust history, that is, to think beyond the assumptions and categories that have structured and continued to limit the historiography and memory of Nazi persecution. The book is a tour de force combining rigorous historical detective work with nuanced historiographic sophistication."

Paul Lerner, Professor and Chair of History, University of Southern California

"Now available in English, *People without History Are Dust* does the vital work of historizing homophobia during the Holocaust and in its memory. Anna Hájková pinpoints the silence in survivor testimony as a calculated disavowal of queer desire to remove its stain on remembrance: an intentional archival absence that she restores with unflinching accounts of the complex and sometimes uncomfortable interplays between queer desire and Jewish experiences of the Shoah. To queer the Holocaust, then, is to refuse to look away."

Zavier Nunn, Assistant Professor of History and Gender and Sexuality Studies, Northwestern University

"A remarkable and brave work of holocaust history, *People without History Are Dust* is the first exploration of the intersection of queerness and Jewishness in the Holocaust. Like Anna Hájková's previous work, this is not the Hollywood version of the Holocaust with neat boundaries and binaries. Instead, Hájková offers us the bare truth: that sex, death, and life intersected in the camps in messy ways still inconvenient for today's mainstream narratives."

Eli Rubin, Professor of History, Western Michigan University

"Carefully researched, innovative, and moving, this is one of the most original contributions to Holocaust Studies of recent years. Anna Hájková makes an insurmountable case for a queer approach to the Holocaust, demonstrating how a focus on what has been marginalized sheds light on the phenomenon as a whole. *People without History Are Dust* is a short book, but a genuinely significant one."

Dan Stone, Professor of Modern History and Director of the Holocaust Research Institute, Royal Holloway, University of London

"This vital book intervenes in the explicit and implicit homophobic erasure of survivors' and scholars' narratives with nuanced case studies that prioritize women and teenagers, to whom Anna Hájková grants what she calls 'historical citizenship' at the intersection of queer acts and Jewish identity. Hajkova excels at uncovering agency even where consent is impossible; her tender and incisive writing positions desire as part of the will to survive."

Mir Yarfitz, Associate Professor of History and Affiliate Faculty in Women's, Gender, and Sexuality Studies, Wake Forest University

Anna Hájková

People without History Are Dust

Queer Desire in the Holocaust

Translated by Anna Hájková
and William Ross Jones

UNIVERSITY OF TORONTO PRESS
Toronto Buffalo London

University of Toronto Press
Toronto Buffalo London
utppublishing.com
© University of Toronto Press 2025

All rights reserved. No part of this publication may be reproduced, stored in or introduced into a retrieval system, or transmitted in any form or by any means (electronic, mechanical, photocopying, recording, or otherwise) without the prior written permission of both the copyright owner and the above publisher of this book.

Library and Archives Canada Cataloguing in Publication

Title: People without history are dust : queer desire in the Holocaust / Anna Hájková; translated by Anna Hájková and William Ross Jones.
Other titles: Menschen ohne Geschichte sind Staub. English
Names: Hájková, Anna, author, translator | Jones, William Ross, translator.
Description: Translation of: Menschen ohne Geschichte sind Staub : Homophobie und Holocaust. | Includes bibliographical references and index.
Identifiers: Canadiana (print) 20250268892 | Canadiana (ebook) 20250268906 | ISBN 9781487557102 (cloth) | ISBN 9781487557119 (paper) | ISBN 9781487557126 (PDF) | ISBN 9781487557140 (EPUB)
Subjects: LCSH: Holocaust, Jewish (1939–1945) | LCSH: Homosexuality. | LCSH: Homophobia. | LCSH: Nazi concentration camps.
Classification: LCC D804.5.G38 H3513 2025 | DDC 940.53/1808664 – dc23

ISBN 978-1-4875-5710-2 (cloth)   ISBN 978-1-4875-5714-0 (EPUB)
ISBN 978-1-4875-5711-9 (paper)   ISBN 978-1-4875-5712-6 (PDF)

Printed in Canada

Cover design: Filip Kraus and Kristjan Buckingham
Cover images: (*clockwise*) Photos of Anne Frank, Nate Leipciger, Margot Heuman, Gad Beck, Sabina Goldman, and Jiří Vrba are courtesy of the Anne Frank House, The Azrieli Foundation, the family of Margot Heuman, United States Holocaust Memorial Museum, and Anna Hájková.

We wish to acknowledge the land on which the University of Toronto Press operates. This land is the traditional territory of the Wendat, the Anishnaabeg, the Haudenosaunee, the Métis, and the Mississaugas of the Credit First Nation.

University of Toronto Press acknowledges the financial support of the Government of Canada, the Canada Council for the Arts, and the Ontario Arts Council, an agency of the Government of Ontario, for its publishing activities.

 Canada Council for the Arts   Conseil des Arts du Canada

 ONTARIO ARTS COUNCIL
CONSEIL DES ARTS DE L'ONTARIO
an Ontario government agency
un organisme du gouvernement de l'Ontario

Funded by the Government of Canada   Financé par le gouvernement du Canada

 MIX
Paper | Supporting responsible forestry
FSC® C103567

Contents

List of Illustrations ix

Foreword xi
Jennifer Evans

Preface xv

1 Towards a Queer History of the Holocaust 1
    The Queer Archival Gap 9
    Homophobia 13
    Gad Beck 22
    Queer Desire in Theresienstadt 35
    Conclusion 50

2 People without History Are Dust 54
    Margot Heuman 59
    Queer Kinship 70

Nate Leipciger 73
Anne Frank 79
Molly Applebaum 89
Jiří Vrba 96
Conclusion 112

Notes 115

Bibliography 131

Index 153

Illustrations

1.1 Irene Miller's partner as "other relationships" 12
1.2 Interview with Linda Breder 17
1.3 Gad Beck, ca. 1943 24
1.4 Gad Beck and Carsten Does, 2006 29
1.5 Fredy Hirsch, late 1930s 41
1.6 Erich Lichtblau, "Hambo, the Pop-Hit Singer" 48
2.1 Źródło samotności, Polish edition of Radclyffe Hall's *The Well of Loneliness* 56
2.2 Margot Heuman, 1946 61
2.3 Margot Heuman and Dita Neumann, 1956 67
2.4 Margot Heuman and Anna Hájková, 2018 69
2.5 Nate Leipciger, September 1945 75
2.6 Anne Frank, 1942 80
2.7 Page from Anne Frank's diary, 1944 81
2.8 Graphic novel adaptation of *The Diary of Anne Frank* by Ari Folman and David Polonsky 85

2.9 Melania Weissenberg, 1942   90
2.10 Sabina Goldman and her sister Mania   93
2.11 Dedication on photo of Goldman sisters   94
2.12 Molly Applebaum with two children, 1950s   95
2.13 Jiří Vrba, 1990s   98
2.14 Jiří Vrba, 1946   101
2.15 Jiří Vrba at Bratislava synagogue, 1989   109

Foreword

One of the most common weapons used to deny the humanity of people in the present is to deny them their past. We have seen this tactic used before. Raul Hilberg had to fight to get his now classic text into print, while for years, historians of women and gender struggled for legitimacy in their quest to write a more inclusive social and cultural history of the Shoah. Often the backlash came from outside the field. Sometimes, regrettably, from within.

The denial of history has at its root a common purpose: to unmake the hard-fought struggles queer people have made – and continue to make – to be part of the social fabric of our world. A focus on lives lived beyond contemporary sexual and gender expectations is often derided as fashionable, presentist, or worse, woke. On some level it seems impossible to understand why expanding the historical record would touch such a nerve. On another, though, it shows just how urgently needed Anna Hájková's important, groundbreaking book is now.

Same-sex sexuality and non-normative gender comportment rankles. It forces us to reckon with our own sense of identity, intimacy, and sometimes, uncomfortable truths. In the aftermath of the Shoah, these stories were often hidden from view and hard to find. Illegality and social shame meant survivors turned to other matters, reconnecting with family and community. They went about the business of rebuilding broken lives. Some of them repressed the traumas they faced in hiding or in the ghettos and camps, only to speak of them later in life. Others stared down family and community pressures and expectations. But as Hájková's book brilliantly shows, in many cases, these stories were there all along. We just failed to ask.

There is, of course, more to this matter of when and how queer and trans histories have surfaced. It would not be wrong to say there has been a lag compared to other fields. Hájková lays out several reasons for this. One is certainly structural, that Holocaust studies have focused the bulk of early attention on systems of perpetration over individual experience. We might add the methodological challenges posed by an overtly empirical discipline when encountering subjective accounts – testimonies, memoirs, and oral histories – sources which offer a lens into more personalized and subjective accounts but that require interdisciplinary approaches that have not always been welcome in this social history–driven field.

Another reason for the slow uptake of queer and trans history – and this is where Hájková is particularly brave – is owed to the lingering stain of homophobia. It was homophobia and internalized shame that made it difficult for Nate Leipciger to disclose his sexual abuse at the hands of another man in the camps. And it is homophobia combined with misogyny that makes it difficult for families and even contemporary audiences to countenance feelings between women in moments of extreme violence. These intimacies, sometimes forged of bartering and abuse, other times of curiosity, fantasy, and love, reveal the limits and possibilities of our individual and collective humanity. They are troubling in the way in which they challenge us to think outside of our comfort zones, and they call into question what we believe we already know. But more fundamentally, they question the romanticization and likeability of some victims and survivors, hinting at malicious intra-victim violence, which for some, shifts the focus away from the "real" perpetrators. Others show us how one might be simultaneously a victim and perpetrator of violence, complicating our picture of the Holocaust.

Yet, as Hájková shows, there is so much to be gained from queering the history of the Holocaust. Aside from a more nuanced portrait of the broad spectrum of experiences in hiding, in the ghettos and camps, and in adjusting to life after 1945, we also bear witness to the alliances that helped people survive. This requires expert handling of the evidence to tease out the various twists and turns in a person's narrative. These accounts challenge us to be better listeners and interlocutors; they challenge us to write better history.

When we do, we find stories that take us beyond the page, offering vital lessons for today. We learn of solidarities and kinships borne of shared, though different, struggles. While historians remain deadlocked in internecine battles over the merits and shortcomings of comparative frameworks for thinking about genocide, some of the survivors portrayed here managed to find common ground. Many, as we also learn, reached across generations to have their stories told with the honesty and urgency that sometimes only comes with age.

Finally, in putting the focus on desire itself, in both its productive and repressive manifestations, Hájková goes where few historians dare to go. This is a very human history. It shows people at their most vulnerable, and sometimes with a measure of youthful precociousness. These biographies offer us complex people with even more complex emotions. We owe them our attention. We owe them their past.

Jennifer Evans

Preface

It is a great privilege, and a rare feat, to have my short book on queer Holocaust history come out in English translation. It happened thanks to the encouragement and confidence of many colleagues around the world. My thanks are in particular to my friend Benjamin Hett who put the idea into my head; and to Jennifer Evans, who inspires me to be the best kind of historian and colleague. Eli Rubin offered not only his feedback, but also invited me to discuss the manuscript with his brilliant graduate students at Western Michigan University. I finished the manuscript while a fellow at the Frankel Center for Judaic Studies at the University of Michigan, where I benefited from the support of the wonderful Maya Barzilai. The German original, *Menschen ohne Geschichte sind Staub*, was written within the deepest part of the pandemic, as the Alpha variant of COVID-19 broke out. In the UK, everything was closed for three months, including swimming pools and libraries, the two focal points of my life. I relied on the kindness of friends, colleagues, and strangers from social media in recommending literature, sending PDFs of their own work, and photographing passages from books. In particular, I am grateful to the Azrieli Foundation and Arielle Berger for their support for this project throughout. I should also express my thanks to Sharon Wrock for sending me new photos of her mother, Molly Applebaum.

I am grateful to Anne Gerritsen, Claudia Gray, and Keri Husband from the Department of History at the University of Warwick for making funds available that paid for the majority of the translation of chapter 2. I was thrilled that the brilliant Will Jones agreed to take the translation on, not least because I am a huge admirer of their work. Their rendition of the original is sensitive and careful. Emma Kühnelt compiled the bibliography, edited footnotes, and worked on the index, which was a huge help. Thanks are due to the Humanities Research Fund at Warwick, which paid for that work.

The book in front of you offers two revised pieces of my older work. The name-giving second half is an expanded translation of *Menschen ohne Geschichte sind Staub* that came out with Wallstein Verlag in June 2021. I updated the literature, conducted the historiographical research I was not able to do three years before, and to the footnotes, added insight for the reader into some of the new scholarship. I added one new chapter, on the Czech survivor Jiří Vrba. Will Jones's scholarship inspired me to reconsider some aspects in the section on Nate Leipciger. The conservative backlash and library bans added a new passage to the Anne Frank section. In brighter news, the Dutch original of the library has been available since September 2021 online, which is how I proceeded here. Since the publication of the original, my friend Margot Heuman passed away in May 2022. She liked the chapter I wrote about her, and I saw the "little yellow book" in her living room when I last visited her in April 2022. Readers who are familiar with the German original will notice that "Emma" has now a different name – her actual name. When Margot was eulogized in the *New York Times*, the journalist used the full maiden name of her girlfriend, Dita Neumann. Margot's son also provided the photo of both women for the article. The change in Dita's name was due to her grandchild, who pressured Margot to keep the name of his (long dead) grandmother out of her story. Margot recognized the homophobia of the request, but followed it. Now Dita can have her name back. On that note: Polish and Czech, like all Slavic languages, usually use diminutives for first names. Sabina becomes Bineczka or Bineńka, Jiří Jirka, or Maria, Mancia, and Mania.

The first chapter serves as an introduction to what queer Holocaust history is and what immense difficulties it has had to overcome, and still often faces. It is based on my essay "Den Holocaust queer erzählen" from *Jahrbuch Sexualitäten* 2018, which I originally wrote in English and translated into German for that publication. It was my first piece of academic writing on queer Holocaust history. I started preparing it for publication in English in 2020, not least thanks to the encouragement of my friend Ervin Malakaj. Due to many things, most of them traumatic, I could not finish. Now, for this book, I could. There are some significant changes in the second half of the essay: following the sterling advice of the reviewers, I wrote a new section on Gad Beck. I have also added a section on Fredy Hirsch. I have also come to acknowledge some of the difficult aspects of queer history, including sexual abuse of teenagers, and addressed them in the sections on Hirsch and Hambo. Following the blossoming of trans history (and an invitation to present at the New York Museum of Jewish Heritage in June 2022 alongside Katie Sutton and Bodie Ashton), I rewrote the section on Hambo the clown as a gender non-conforming person. I have cut the section on Anneliese Kohlmann, since I have published about her in *German History* and am writing a book. I also removed the section on homophobic attacks on myself, to make the essay less about me, and more about the past.

This book would not have been possible without the unwavering support of my editor, Stephen Shapiro. He has been helpful and encouraging the entire time. Thanks to working with him, the process of writing this book never felt mystifying or hard. One reason why I worked hard to write the best book I possibly could was to make Stephen proud. I am very grateful for the constructive and clear feedback from the two anonymous reviewers. Thank you, whoever you are.

I signed the contract for this book in the summer of 2023. This was the summer that I will always remember as that of the two weddings to my wife, Albane Duvillier, a legal one in London, our home, and a social one in Prague, where our marriage is not recognized. Albane's love has taught me to pay attention to the present, to hold fewer grudges, and to cherish what I have. As I worked on this book throughout the fall, I reflected on the often-sad nature of the content and the happiness of my life. That is a tremendous privilege, making me close with a smile and love.

CHAPTER ONE

Towards a Queer History of the Holocaust

How can we, in a useful way, queer the history of the Holocaust? This question has not been posed before.[1] This chapter offers the first original exploration of queer Holocaust history, that is, same-sex desire between Jews persecuted by the Nazis as Jews, who were imprisoned in ghettos and concentration camps. It is a difficult story to write: the society of the Holocaust's victims was characterized by extensive homophobia that depicted the people who engaged in same-sex desire as repulsive. This prejudice brought about the stigmatization of queerness, effectively silencing survivors who could have spoken about same-sex experience. This chapter maps homophobia in survivor testimonies, its impact on scholarly literature and memory alike, and the subsequent archival erasure of queer experience. It also offers examples of how to map the queer biographies of Holocaust victims.

Telling their stories is, however, not an easy goal. The overwhelming majority of mentions of queer desire in survivors' testimonies is homophobic. Most often, queer people who come up in survivors' testimonies were depicted as dangerous, deviant, even monstrous – always as "other" from the narrator. Testifying is a social act: that means that we tell our lives within the framework of the socially acceptable. This stigmatization of same-sex desire led to the fact that almost no Holocaust survivors who engaged in same-sex desire, or those who self-identified as gay or lesbian, told their own story or, if they did, discussed their own queer sexuality.

In the last three decades, German history has been actively researched from a queer perspective, first as a history of homosexuality, then also as queer history.[2] Nevertheless, the consideration of a queer Holocaust history is absent. Scholars have investigated influential members of the German queer movement, such as Magnus Hirschfeld and Martha Mosse, both Jews and victims of National Socialist persecution. However, barring such outstanding personalities, the categories of Jewishness and queerness have been thought of as distinctly separate. It was as if all persecuted homosexuals were non-Jews, while all Jewish victims were heterosexual. That these two groups could have intersected – in fact, must have intersected – has never been raised. This lack of recognition of an intersectionality of queer Jewish Holocaust victims is salient in its own right. I suggest we need to critique this thinking in fossilized categories and question what this perspective brings about.[3]

Where did this homophobia come from? Given the push to liberalize and decriminalize homosexuality in many interwar European countries, the prejudice comes as a surprise, especially given its fierceness and prominence.[4] Why did people who were persecuted, whose families were exterminated, who were forced to perform back-breaking labour and exposed to physical violence, starvation, and dirt, feel disgusted and threatened by same-sex relationships? What is even more remarkable is that this revulsion did not only apply to queer desire expressed towards the narrating survivor, but to the much more frequent occurrence of witnessing a same-sex couple in their vicinity.[5] It is significant that Holocaust victims apparently felt more tormented by queer sexuality than by heterosexual sexual violence.[6] This marking of queerness as monstrous has had an impact on what could be remembered, narrated, and collected; what found its way into the Holocaust archive; and what in turn was seen as suitable history.[7]

This chapter explores these silenced queer histories. By writing a history of people seen as so deviant that they are best left out, I explore larger issues of how normatively Holocaust history has been told. Here, my work follows a second approach to "queering" the Holocaust. My goal is not only to add queer Jews to the history of the Shoah. Queering a history means reading from the margins, asking about what is missing, about what happens in the shadows, about the hidden things nobody wants to see, in short, thinking about the power hierarchies the sources we read serve. Jennifer Evans famously summarized: "To queer the past is to view it sceptically, to pull apart its constitutive pieces and analyse them from a variety of perspectives, taking nothing for granted."[8]

Following this approach, I emphasize what perspective was served when the queer experience was left out: queer Holocaust history helps to recognize the redemptive narrative in which this genocide is often told. Analysing sexuality, including queer sexuality, redirects our attention away from the expectation for unrealistic – and ahistorical – heroes and saints. Many of the sexual and romantic relationships that took place in the Holocaust – be it relationships between rescuers and Jews in hiding, prisoners in the concentration camps, or inmates in ghettos – were marked by hierarchies and exploitation. In the horrifying world of the camps, sexuality had many functions – comfort, spare time activity, social contract, and resource – but it was also a statement of power. Power hierarchies were so defining in almost all sexual and romantic relationships in the concentration camps that sexuality in fact presents a place where we can observe how prisoner society exercised power. Status needs to be performed, which is why the sex life had to be visible to be recognized as status marker. Access to sexuality became a way of demonstrating one's status.[9] Observing sex as a mechanism of power also meant that the weaker partners who engaged in sexual barter were often coerced. These relationships, often violent, were between prisoner functionaries, or even perpetrators, and dependent inmates.

What this chapter does not present is an exhaustive overview of queer experiences in the Holocaust – that would not be possible, even in an entire monograph! It also does not explore one of the best known, and possibly very frequent instances, of queer sex in the camps, that is the violent relationships between prisoner functionaries and the "pipel," their coerced young partners.[10] (The situation of pipel is discussed in the second chapter, in the section on Nate Leipciger.) Similarly, this chapter does not explore enforced queer relationships between Jewish inmates and guards.

Queer Holocaust history is an independent field of research that emerged from two much larger historiographies, namely that of Nazi persecution of queer and trans people, and that of Jewish Holocaust history. The history of queer desire in the Holocaust does not seek to contribute to our understanding of the Nazi persecution. Many scholars have focused on exploring the specific nature of Nazi persecution against the Romani, gays and lesbians, or the disabled for who they were; these are important and obvious histories. My approach is different: in exploring queerness as a subjectivity experienced by the Jewish victims persecuted by the Nazis due to their race, I write a victim-centred history.

The combination of these two lines of inquiry, on queerness and the Holocaust, changes the questions asked, the backdrop, and the sources. Let me give an example: in insightful analyses, Kim Wünschmann and Albert Knoll wrote about Jewish prisoners in early concentration camps who had been arrested as homosexuals, whose situation was particularly vulnerable in their intersectional markers as pink triangle prisoners **and** Jews.[11] The systematic deportations of Central European Jews started in October 1941; the people I write about were deported from their homes from December 1941 on. By the time in fall 1941 that the SS deported Jewish victims for their race, the situation in the concentration camps was very different, and the conditions were even more dreadful. The camps were far larger, and there were far more of them; some prisoner functionaries established system of sexual abuse of the pipel. Most importantly, from July 1942 on, the gas chambers in Auschwitz started methodologically murdering the arriving Jews. The research on the Nazi persecution of gay men in Germany and Austria has produced a solid body of publications that discuss the method the police and Gestapo used, the numbers of men persecuted, or role of the denunciations.[12] In contrast, the situation of these men in the concentration camps is somewhat less well examined,[13] while the research on the situation of queer women in the camps is fragmentary.[14] It is to this point, the specific queer experience and surviving in the camp society, that my work hopes to contribute.

What are we to call people who engaged in same-sex physical intimacy during the Holocaust? It would be reductive to label them "homosexual," "gay," or "lesbian."[15] Only a fraction of the men and women who engaged in same-sex intimacy in the camps identified as such before or, if they survived, after their incarceration. Because the camps were largely monosexual spaces, if one wanted to be sexually active, members of one's own sex were the only people available.[16] Some of the people who engaged in same-sex intimacy in the camps also engaged in queer intimacy before or after imprisonment. This is probably more often the case for same-sex conduct in mixed-sex camps and ghettos. But few of these people understood themselves as "homosexual."[17] How people made sense of their same-sex attraction and whether they understood it as an identity changed over time, situation, and location.[18]

I use the term "queer" to denote people who engaged in same-sex activity in the camps, without making statements about their self-definition in terms of sexual orientation.[19] These men and women were not always gay, but they are very much part of queer history. In this sense, the adjective "queer" serves here as a collective umbrella term for *acts and practices* rather than a statement on who these people *were*.[20] Similarly, trans history and the history of gender non-conforming persons reminds us of the need to not assume firm gender roles and sex binaries.[21] My insistence on giving up an ahistorical search for homosexual identities and instead writing a history about queer desire and acts is admittedly a topic that is often challenging for readership outside of queer history. "Are we not outing people?" listeners occasionally ask at my lectures and those of many colleagues. I explain that this is an ahistorical question that reduces same-sex intimacy to an assumption of sexual identity. The discussion of Gad Beck and his lovers below is instructive here. I would like to add: it is also the task of every historian to write about what they find in the archives, and not pick and choose suitable histories.

Homophobia that comes up so often in these histories also needs historicizing. It would be ahistorical to measure the values of a past society with our modern eyes. But to assume that "in those times, everyone was homophobic" is not helpful to understand the past. Analysing historical homophobia is akin to studying antisemitism: the fact that in the past it was part of social discourse does not mean we should not examine it critically.[22] Taking the gay rights movements of the interwar era in Germany, Czechoslovakia, Hungary, and Poland into consideration, we see how historical, gender-specific, class, religious, and local differences in homophobic attitudes played out. For instance, Poland decriminalized homosexuality in 1932, thirty-five years prior to Great Britain.[23] Of course, decriminalization did not mean that people stopped being homophobic, but it is still an important historical indication to take into account. Rather than operating under assumptions of continuities of "backwards" Eastern Europe, a close observation of what homophobia meant, what ends it served, and how it emerged aids us in understanding the mechanisms that made homophobia such an important part of prisoner society mentality.[24]

The homophobia in the concentration camps was a new kind, separate from the "old" one as well as that of the Nazis. Insa Eschebach and Uta Rautenberg have argued that prisoner homophobia was an extreme form of othering. For instance, queer women were depicted as disgusting, over-sexualized, and viragos. They were always described as residing in a different prisoner category than the narrator, as "asocial" or "criminal" prisoners and with a different national background. Eschebach has argued that the sexualization of the figure of the "lesbian" created distance between the self and the world of the camps, with all that was wrong with that world.[25] Elizabeth Stephens explains why society marks queer persons as monstrous: meeting a monster is to experience an encounter with the strange.[26] Queer bodies are thus beasts that remind society of the strangeness and queerness of life itself. These insights serve particularly well to explain why in the chaotic, violent world of the camps, marking queer inmates as monsters was a means of familiarizing and ordering. We know that same-sex desire in the Soviet Gulag brought about similar prejudice.[27]

This chapter consists of four parts. The first section examines the queer archival gap. The second explores homophobia in survivor testimonies and how it influenced Holocaust scholarship. The third examines a well-known example of a queer Holocaust survivor, the vivacious Berliner Gad Beck. The fourth discusses traces of queer desire in the Theresienstadt ghetto and the possibility of researching queer biographies.

The Queer Archival Gap

Among the tens, perhaps hundreds, of thousands of testimonies by Holocaust survivors there are next to no explicitly queer voices. There are dozens of Holocaust archives with collections of self-narrated testimonies and oral histories, and yet among these there are next to no first-person testimonies of people who willingly engaged in same-sex intimacy and spoke about it. The four known exceptions are all German Jewish men who experienced the persecution as teenagers or young men and whose testimonies exist as published memoirs. The first and best known is the Berlin resistance fighter Gad Beck (*1923).[28] Less well-known are two young German emigrants to the Netherlands who survived their deportation to the concentration camps, Gerald

Rosenstein (*1927) and Walter Guttmann (*1928).[29] Only one lesbian, Frieda Belinfante (*1904), a "half-Jewish" Dutch resistance fighter, bore testimony.[30] In fact, while the last thirty years have been a fruitful era for feminist Holocaust scholarship, producing much nuanced and careful work, queer women's experiences are entirely missing.[31] Survivors talking about queer sexual violence are rare, but present.[32]

The absence of queer voices is striking for two reasons: first, the Holocaust is a genocide that has been extensively documented in terms of oral history interviews. Second, bearing witness was for survivors a meaningful reaction to coming to terms with mass violence.[33] There are testimonies from nearly everyone, even magicians or people in mental asylums.[34] Even people who experienced matters long considered too traumatic to speak about, such as victims of sexual violence or parents who killed their children, have given testimony.[35]

One can observe the omission of queer experience in the case of the USC Shoah Foundation, which runs the Visual History Archive (VHA). The VHA is the world's largest archive of oral histories and perhaps the largest collection of any witness testimonies of the Shoah. The VHA has over fifty-two thousand interviews with people who were persecuted as Jews. In addition to this collection, they also hold interviews with other victim groups: victims of Armenian and Rwandan genocides, "Righteous among Nations" (non-Jews who rescued Jews during the Holocaust), and six gay gentile men persecuted under Nazi Germany's Paragraph 175. The interviews have all been keyworded, so a researcher can use the keywords to search for specific places or themes rather than looking through hundreds of thousands of hours of oral histories. There are keywords for homosexuality, homosexual kapo, and much more – some one thousand keywords altogether. But every single instance of testimony linked to these keywords leads to statements of outright homophobia. With the exception of Gad Beck, the largest oral history archive of Jewish Holocaust survivors does not have a single voice who explicitly spoke about his or her same-sex desire.[36]

In 2010, I realized the existence of this gap. I reached out to the colleagues at the VHA to address this silence. But these conversations turned out to be difficult.[37] The colleagues repeatedly pointed out the existence of those six interviews with gay gentile survivors. I started to understand that influential categorization, in which all persecuted homosexuals were non-Jews and all Jewish victims were heterosexual; queerness and Jewish Holocaust victims did not overlap. This categorization was so embedded that it made my point about queer Holocaust survivors incommunicable. Luckily, however, over the last few years, the VHA has undergone a change, and they are now starting to address queer histories of the Holocaust.

Through my research, I was able to find out that among the interviewees were in fact Holocaust survivors who willingly engaged in queer sex as well as those who identified as gay and lesbian. It was the framing of the interview, I believe, its heteronormative framework, that prevented survivors from mentioning their same-sex experience. This is particularly unfortunate, since most of the VHA interviews took place between 1994 and 1999, a quarter of a century after the Stonewall riots, the decriminalization of

Segment#: 146
working life
Helene Miller – daughters

Segment#: 147
Joanne* – other relationships

Figure 1.1. Irene Miller's partner described as "other relationships."

homosexuality in Germany, and the publication of the first well-known gay survivor memoir.[38]

A specific technique of queer erasure can be observed in the interview of Irene Miller, a "half-Jewish" lesbian Ravensbrück survivor and resistance fighter from Prague, that she gave to the Jewish Family and Children's Services.[39] Throughout her interview, Miller tried to mention her sexual orientation and her partner. Her interviewer, a man, never let her: he would change the topic or say he was interested in something else. Perhaps he did not even register what Miller was trying to say because he did not recognize it as relevant, being fixated on a heteronormative framework.[40] In the keywords, Miller's partner Joanne is keyworded as "other relationship."[41] When Miller was interviewed by lesbian scholars such as Christa Schikorra, she indicated that this was her sexual orientation and referred to her queer biography.[42]

Stories such as these draw our attention to the influence of social expectations and the key role of the interviewer.[43] For queer content, the people leading the oral histories too often reacted to mentions of queer intimacy with redirecting questions that normalized homophobia. Scholars of Holocaust testimonies have focused on the boundaries of the narratable that are dictated by the social expectations of the public or on the unbearable.[44] We should also pay attention to normative expectations of the interviewers who made bearing testimony impossible, or at least very hard.[45] Part of this normativity was the homophobia of the interviewers, a prejudice that they possibly brought in from their understanding of queer inmates as deviant figures.

The final scene in the VHA interviews was yet another factor that made narrating a queer biography difficult. At this moment, the survivor was joined by his or her spouse, children, and grandchildren. This scene staged a happy ending as a familial triumph over the destruction of the Holocaust. But this framing staged success as exclusively heteronormative, making it impossible to tell a story of a happy, queer life. While this ending is specific to the VHA, it serves as a useful indicator of the impact of normativity in Holocaust oral history collections writ large. The childless, unmarried homosexual survivor was by this logic a social failure and thus not fit to bear witness.

Homophobia

What did survivor homophobia look like? I will demonstrate with two examples from the VHA. Sientje Backer was a Dutch Jewish woman born in 1914 in Amsterdam as Sientje Stibbe. Backer's war odyssey was as tragic as it was dramatic. In 1942, she was a married woman and mother of two little children, whom she was able to send into hiding. Backer herself was deported to Vught, Westerbork, and in 1943, Auschwitz. Here she became a victim of forced medical experiments by Carl Clauberg, who injected her uterus with a caustic substance.[46] She was never able to have children again. At the evacuation of Auschwitz in January 1945, Backer was sent to Ravensbrück and from there on a death march a few months later to its satellite camp, Neustadt-Glewe. The women were forced to march through knee-high snow; those who could not keep up the tempo were shot. "That was a terrible, terrible time." Backer described her arrival in the main camp:

> When we came to Ravensbrück, yes, I was of course soaked. When we went to bed, I was scared sick. I didn't dare to go to sleep because I was scared of all the lesbians. [leans forward] I was TERRIFIED. I cannot tell you how terrified I was. And I didn't dare to go to sleep. But I must have dozed off anyways. Because when I woke up my yellow stockings were gone. [laughs heartily] My yellow stockings. My yellow stockings were gone. They had stolen them, they liked them I think.[47]

At this point, her interviewer asked Backer something completely different. The interviewer eschewed any logical follow-up questions, such as why Backer was so terrified of the lesbians or the importance of the yellow stockings. In the sequence describing the horrifying time of the last months before liberation, the lesbian prisoners come in the same context as the exhausting march in the cold and snow without appropriate clothing. Backer's one piece of suitable clothing were the yellow stockings; in an earlier remark she notes that she even did not have underpants. Significantly, in the moment when Backer emphasized the horrific in her narrative (not only in words, but in the volume and tone of her voice, and her posture), she inserted lesbian prisoners. Among the many profoundly traumatic experiences in her persecution biography, including the separation from her children and the forced medical experiments, it was the queer women whom she singled out as particularly threatening. Backer offered no explanation why she found the queer inmates so terrifying. But in not asking, the interviewer allowed for logic in which it seems obvious that lesbian prisoners would be scary. Backer's narration of the terrifying other follows Insa Eschebach's argument on the artificial construction of the monstrous, frightening lesbian. Finally, the laughter punctuating Backer's narrative was not meant to soften her harsh words describing the lesbians. She laughed only a few times throughout the interview, seemingly to mark the frequent absurdity of the persecution and the unknowability of the things that happened to the prisoners.

Linda Breder's interview offers an example in which the role of the homophobic interviewer is transformative. Born in 1924 as Libuše Reichová in Stropkov, Slovakia, she was among the few thousand young Jewish women who were deported to Auschwitz-Birkenau with the first Slovak transports.[48] At one point in the interview, she mentioned, without prodding:

> Although we had in Birkenau also lesbians I can say homosexuals because I was ... which I knew von [unclear] she is

still alive and very good friend of mine ... she was a physician in Auschwitz, too. Doctor Manci Schwalbová, ... and I know one Reichsdeutsche Politische [German political prisoner] with whom she was very good friends and it was rumours that they were lesbians. Then I know kapos, the German kapos, which were also rumours. But I can, I didn't have, I mean, any experience from the Jewish girls which were, you know, close, at our work or in the barracks with me that I know about, but I know it was rumours that there are homosexuals there.

Q: Did these homosexual – lesbian kapos ever hit upon [sic] the inmates?
A: Probably they did, I don't know because I always had the same kapo. And working in the unit that I was, she never hit us.
Q: Not hit, I mean, try to seduce some of the [unclear]?
A: I don't know, I don't know. This, in this field, I really don't know. If somebody from the Germans was a homosexual hit [sic] or she wasn't, but mostly they were very cruel. So hard to say. Hard to say.[49]

Breder's clip is particularly rich because it offers various takes on queer desire. It starts with a sympathetic portrayal of a lesbian prisoner, the well-known prisoner doctor Manci Schwalbová, a fellow Slovak Jew.[50] Other survivors also recalled that Schwalbová was queer.[51] It is worth noting that here Breder outed Schwalbová, who never openly spoke about her sexuality. Breder also defined Schwalbová's sexual orientation through rumours in the camp that her friend,

Towards a Queer History of the Holocaust | 17

Figure 1.2. Still photo of Linda Breder talking about lesbian prisoners. USC Shoah Foundation.

a German political prisoner, was in fact Schwalbová's lover. Breder then continued to catalogue other queer women, also defined by rumours, who were German prisoner functionaries. Importantly, she mentioned her own group of "Jewish girls" as one in which she was not aware of anyone being queer. But here, Breder contradicts herself: Schwalbová was Jewish and was deported on the same transports in spring 1942 from Slovakia as Breder. Schwalbová was one of Breder's "Jewish girls" and she was queer. But because Breder was friends with her, she did not describe Schwalbová directly as a lesbian; instead, she alluded to it as "rumours," which she did bring up.[52] This narrative strategy allowed

Breder to gossip about her queer friend, but to keep her as a friend, within her own group. That her depiction of queer German prisoners is presented in contrast to the Jews represents a form of othering.

At this point, the interviewer stepped in and asked whether the queer women ever tried to "hit on someone." In fact, the interviewer misspoke the phrase as "hit upon" – possibly she misspoke because she was nervous, as one does when discussing a sensitive topic. This question moved what had so far been described as queer intimacy into potential sexual violence, applying scripting. The phrase the interviewer used, "hit on someone," denotes one party making sexual advances to another, which implies sexual harassment or abuse. The interviewer's question framed the lesbians as sexually dominant, echoing the notion of the lesbian predator.[53] Breder's English was not entirely perfect; she emigrated to the US in 1968. She misunderstood the colloquial phrase "to hit on" as "to hit," responding that her kapo did not beat the women in her working group. The interviewer rephrased the question, and the otherwise very talkative Breder replied that she did not know. But at this point she added that the kapos were "very cruel." The misinterpreted word "hit" introduced violence into the interview; the interviewer interrupted and changed the line of thought Breder was pursuing. While Breder started on an open-minded note on Schwalbová's sexuality, the interview section ended implying that apart from her, the lesbians were German, kapos, and behaved with cruelty.

These homophobic statements and assumptions were repeated in the first standard histories of concentration camps that were largely written by survivors. The homophobic statements in these early important history books were almost never questioned. One such example can be seen in *The Death Factory*, an early standard work on Auschwitz written by Erich Kulka and Ota Kraus, two Czech Jews arrested for being in the resistance. (Incidentally, Breder and Kulka were friends.) A part of the book offers a glossary of camp terms, one of which reads: "Pink triangle. Worn by persons imprisoned for sexual perversion or homosexuality (*Schwule Brüder*). In the camps they had a splendid opportunity to corrupt the maximum number of young lads."[54] The entry ascribed the practice of the sexual abuse of teenage prisoners, informally called "pipel" in the camps, assistants of kapos who often also forced the teenagers to have sex.[55] But the authors were mixing up groups. Most of the prisoners who were in positions of power were not persecuted homosexuals, who in fact were at the bottom of the social hierarchy in the camps.[56] The kapos who kept pipel and subjected them to sexual abuse were in the overwhelming majority men who were arrested for reasons other than homosexuality.[57] Kulka and Kraus must have been aware of this difference,[58] and their mixing up of both groups served as a form of marking queer desire as deviant and abusive.

Hermann Langbein, a "half-Jewish" Austrian Communist, was the author of the classic account *People in Auschwitz*. Langbein was imprisoned in Auschwitz between 1942 and 1944, where he was forced to work as a clerk in the infirmary. After the liberation, he headed the International Auschwitz Committee and played an important role organizing survivors to act as witnesses at the Auschwitz

Trial in Frankfurt am Main. His discussion of queer desire exclusively focuses on sexual abuse of minors:

> A remedy for sexual distress that was customary in other concentration camps, in which no women were interned next to men, was frequently used in Auschwitz as well. Capos kept Pipel, young fellows who in return for personal services were exempted from hard labor and enjoyed other privileges. Quite a number of capos abused their boys sexually. ... Abraham Matuszak reports that what functionaries in Auschwitz did with their Pipel cried to high heaven. If the boys were not willing, they were sent the way of all flesh.[59]

Langbein's depiction of the sexual abuse in these hierarchical, exploitative relationships was more accurate than that of Kraus and Kulka. However, Langbein's choice to focus on the pipel practice only contributed to an understanding of queer intimacy as exclusively abusive and linked it to pedophilia, an established pattern to pathologize queer desire. *People in Auschwitz* was reissued in 2004 without any comment on this passage, either in the editor's introduction or a commenting footnote to this passage.[60]

Several of the historians of this generation simply listed homosexuals as part of a group of the so-called unworthy victims. The US historian Lucy Dawidowicz was not a survivor herself, but lived in Vilna before the war and was part of the social circles of many people who went on to survive the Holocaust. Dawidowicz mentioned in one breath "prostitutes, homosexuals, perverts, and common criminals" when describing those deported alongside the Jews.[61] She wrote this as late as 1981. By this point, the first scholars of the persecution of gay men had begun to take issue with this portrayal.[62] Other survivors-turned-scholars offered a more balanced view. The sociologist Anna Pawełczynska acknowledged the existence of "authentic, emotional relationships" and "mutual love" among same-sex partners.[63] But then she continued: "Sometimes a confirmed homosexual would lead a prisoner of normal [sic] inclinations into homosexual practices. Such arrangements were usually deeply immoral or deeply demoralizing." She also described queer intimacy as "pederastic sexual needs."[64] Pawełczynska operated under the notion of "situational homosexuality" and an assumption that those who are not "really" homosexual are "seduced."[65] Her perspective suggests that the "hard" homosexual was abnormal and that his or her relationship with a different prisoner was immoral and "pederastic." The linking of same-sex desire to pedophilia has been traditionally used as a tool to stigmatize queerness.

This homophobia continued to shape current scholarship until just a few years ago.[66] Sarah Helm, the author of a trade monograph on Ravensbrück, continued in this line of othering queer experience as sexually deviant. In one passage, she gently reproached an elderly survivor, Wanda Połtawska, for the homophobia in her memoir.[67] But elsewhere Helm stated that female guards were motivated to work in Ravensbrück for sexual reasons. Some were there to meet "handsome officers, while for those who were lesbians – a significant minority – Ravensbrück offered special opportunities to meet other women," basing this sweeping statement on a single survivor account.[68] One form of homophobic othering was the sexualization of female perpetrators, ascribing to them sexual perversion and equating it with queer desire.[69] Helm was aware of survivors' homophobic narratives, and in her book, discussed raising the issue when visiting Połtawska as an old lady.[70] It is unfortunate that Helm could not avoid homophobic prejudice herself when it came to describing the guards.

What should we do with these sections of scholarly books published in the past? I do not think we should remove these passages from their accounts. But we should not let them stand without commentary, as it would continue the stigmatization and thus contribute to problematic research, both intellectually and ethically. Ota Kraus, Erich Kulka, Wanda Połtawska, and Hermann Langbein were courageous, brave antifascists. In their homophobia they were symptomatic of the prisoner society. In our search for a more inclusive history, we need to embrace their ambivalences.

Gad Beck

Gad Beck is probably the best-known queer Holocaust survivor, and with a good reason: his memoir, first published in 1995 in German and four years later in English, has brought lasting attention to his story.[71] The book has become a popular favourite because Beck's story is fascinating, he is explicit about his queer love and sex life, and he has a sunny outlook on life. The book is also superbly written, with an eye to drama and story development.

Beck moved to Israel after the liberation. He returned to West Berlin in 1979 and started speaking to a wider audience about his queer biography during the Holocaust after 1989, when he began giving guided tours through Berlin's Scheunenviertel.[72] He was also featured in Lutz van Dijk's account of gay biographies, which first came out in 1992.[73] Beck also gave oral history interviews to the German Resistance Memorial Center in 1990, to the United States Holocaust Memorial Museum (USHMM) in 1994, and to the VHA in 1996 and 1998.[74] The man who made the memoir possible was the author, translator, and publisher Frank Heibert. The two got along very well, and their mutual sympathy as well as the fact that Heibert was gay made for an open and trusting atmosphere. Heibert served as a ghostwriter for the memoir as Beck was not a talented writer; Heibert's role is acknowledged as "editor." During their cooperation over eight months, Beck recorded tapes where he narrated his life, which Heibert transcribed and edited. Once there was a draft of the book, Heibert also interviewed the other key protagonists of the memoir, including Beck's sister Miriam Rosenberg, Heinz Abrahamsohn/Zvi Aviram, Jizchak Schwersenz, and Oskar Löwenstein. The accounts overlapped and Miriam Rosenberg praised the result: "My brother hasn't written a line of this text, and yet I hear him from every sentence."[75] The book was originally published in a series that Heibert co-edited for Edition diá, was featured on two tv shows, and once it was reprinted by the popular paperback press dtv, its reputation as a classic was

Figure 1.3. Photo of Gad Beck, ca. 1943. United States Holocaust Memorial Museum.

cemented. In 1999, a translation by Allison Brown came out with the University of Wisconsin Press. Thirty years after its original publication, the book still sells in both English and German; the English edition is one of the press's bestsellers.[76]

Gad Beck was born in 1923 in Berlin alongside his twin sister Miriam. Their parents were a mixed couple, the father a Viennese Jew, the mother a Berliner non-Jew who converted to Judaism. Both children grew up as part of the Jewish community, which made them, in the eyes of the Nazis, into *Geltungsjuden*, that is mixed-race Jews (*Mischlinge*) who were considered Jewish. Maria von der Heydt demonstrated that *Geltungsjuden*, especially after 1942, were often able to avoid the deportations, were deported later, and then to the "preferential" destination of Theresienstadt.[77] It was Beck's status as *Geltungsjude* that was a huge advantage – he needed to go into hiding only relatively late in fall 1944.

As a teenager, Beck was drawn into the Zionist youth movement. He was aware of his queerness from an early age, and was able to engage in a number of sexual encounters. Through his Zionist engagement, Beck also met the closeted gay Zionist youth leader and teacher Jizchak Schwersenz, born in 1915. Another contact was Manfred Lewin who became Beck's great love. In fall 1942, the Lewins were arrested. Gad was able to trick the authorities into having his lover released, but Manfred refused to let his family go without him. They were deported to Auschwitz and murdered.[78]

Following the Factory Action in February 1943, when most of the remaining Jews of Berlin were arrested and sent to Auschwitz, Jizchak Schwersenz, who already had gone into hiding, created Chug Chaluzi, Hebrew for The Circle of Pioneers. The Beck siblings joined and became the core of about fifteen mostly young Jews, *Mischlinge*, and *Geltungsjuden*, who met for religious celebrations, Hebrew classes, outings to the Grunewald Forest, and, crucially, provided support for those members who had gone into hiding. There were several dozen loosely attached members.[79] In June and October 1943, two members of the core were arrested: Edith Wolff, a key organizer, and Leopold Chones, a nineteen-year-old who was tortured but revealed nothing to the Gestapo and was murdered in Auschwitz. Schwersenz was hit hard by these losses, especially that of Chones, who was his lover. He became depressed, withdrew as leader, and in early 1944, was able to escape to Switzerland. From then on, Gad Beck headed the group and focused on helping people go into hiding and providing for them, which meant organizing apartments, food, and false papers that all needed to be paid for. Thanks to the Swiss connection via Schwersenz, Beck was able to receive considerable funding from the Zionist organizations represented by Nathan Schwalb. Beck also engaged in sexual barter with non-Jewish men who provided accommodation for his wards. Beck described a number of sexual and romantic relationships during this time: perhaps the most important one was with Heinz Abrahamsohn (later Zvi Aviram), a sixteen-year-old Jew who escaped deportation in February 1943; an affair with Oskar Löwenstein, a fellow *Geltungsjude*; and another with a fellow Italian POW, as well as others. In fall 1944, Beck himself had gone into hiding. In early March 1945, Beck and Abrahamsohn were arrested, held in the collection camp at Iranische Straße, but were able to survive until the liberation.

After the war, Beck and his family moved to Palestine. Abrahamsohn joined Beck in 1948, and the two lived together in a small house until about the mid-1950s. It is not clear whether their romantic relationship continued or if they lived as friends.[80] In 1968, Abrahamsohn got married to a woman and changed his last name to Aviram.[81]

Holocaust historians are often frustrated with Beck, who has a reputation as an unreliable narrator. In fact, his exuberant storytelling became the subject of a documentary movie, *The Story of Gad Beck* (*Die Freiheit des Erzählens: Das Leben des Gad Beck*).[82] In it, Beck's friend and erstwhile lover casts grave doubts on the iconic story of Beck's rescue of his boyfriend, Manfred Lewin: "not a word of it is true!"[83] The historian Martina Voigt told me that Beck liked to embellish: she saw him tell the same stories over time, and observed how he adorned the anecdotes.[84] Other than that, it is difficult to find further evidence; for many stories, Beck is the only source. My own impression, in having studied the key testimonies by Beck, Aviram, Schwersenz, and Löwenstein, is that they confirm one another.

There is, however, one discrepancy – that of queerness. Neither Schwersenz's nor Aviram's nor Löwenstein's stand-alone testimonies acknowledge their queer experiences.[85] Aviram and Löwenstein stressed that Beck liked to exaggerate – possibly to accommodate his claim that they had been lovers.[86] In the documentary *The Story of Gad Beck*, the film-makers asked Löwenstein directly about "homosexuality," and he acknowledged that indeed, he and Beck had had sex. In the film, Löwenstein was not at ease and yet reacted almost flirtatiously. With a chuckle, he asked: "do you want to hear far-reaching intimacies?" However, the directors recalled that Löwenstein shared the details about his intimate relationship with Beck freely.[87] He also framed his experience with Beck as one of seduction by an older man directed at a younger one without any sexual experience, contrasting with Beck's portrayal in which Löwenstein initiated the relationship, "quickly knew what he wanted," and even saw it as "first big love."[88] We also need to acknowledge that Beck outed Schwersenz as a closeted gay man, and also gave the names of Aviram and Löwenstein as two men with whom he had sex, while he knew that they identified as heterosexual and chose never to speak about their relationships. That was, I should note, a violent decision by Beck that Heibert tried to talk him out of.[89] Schwersenz, Löwenstein, and two other men were outraged when the book came out. They considered applying for an interim injunction against the book and decided against it only because it would have been too expensive. They settled on writing to Heibert demanding changes.[90] In the end, there was only one change regarding queerness that was implemented in the second edition.[91] This passage concerned a portrayal that Schwersenz, a youth leader, allegedly flirted with his pupils and engaged in improper relationships: "He was very intimate with his boys, sometimes he would pull one of them into a corner, whispered with him, gave him a little kiss. He really loved them, and they adored him. During the trips and outings there were constantly moments of closeness. Whenever he became particularly close with one pupil, the others learned of it immediately, and there were jealous scenes."[92] These passages echo the analysis of historians of the German youth movement.[93] The final emended passage is more ambiguous and can be read as "only" jealous scenes among teenage boys fighting over the attentions of a charismatic teacher.

Oskar Löwenstein was unhappy about having the information about his relationship with Beck made public, but did not insist on that fact being removed. Instead, Löwenstein demanded a change in details about the job his father held – a metonymic defence mechanism. Aviram said nothing at all, at least nothing that is in the public record. One can wonder whether Aviram, who emigrated to Israel,

Figure 1.4. Photo of Gad Beck and Carsten Does, 2006.
Source: Courtesy of Carsten Does.

hoped that the memoir, not available in Hebrew, would not cross paths with his family.[94] When he consented to be interviewed for the documentary *The Story of Gad Beck* (*Die Freiheit des Erzählens: Das Leben des Gad Beck*), Aviram did so under the condition that the film-makers would not touch on his and Gad Beck's romantic relationship.[95]

This not complaining was but a temporary truce: in 2007 and 2008, Viola Rautenberg, then a graduate student, interviewed the surviving members of Chug Chaluzi. She argued that they "were not enthusiastic to be asked about the queer factor in the group: the general taboo, the fear that the connection of Jewish resistance with homosexuality could bring it into ridicule, besmirch their names and that of the perished members but also the fact that Chug was not a gay group and that this aspect therefore shouldn't dominate the discussion on the group were expressed."[96] When asked about same-sex desire, so prominent in the memoir of their leader that made this otherwise minor resistance group world-famous, the survivors (who often owed their lives to Beck) saw queerness as a stain on their reputation. In 2012, Gad Beck, who suffered from memory loss during the last years of his life, passed away.

Three years later, in 2015, Aviram published his memoir, edited by two Holocaust historians. Aviram did not name his relationship with Beck as romantic or sexual. However, he described certain incidents, such as the extreme lengths to which Beck went to find him after Aviram escaped from an erstwhile capture, Beck's knowledge of his body, and Beck's arranging to have a dentist replace the front teeth Aviram lost during Gestapo torture.[97] In my opinion, these moments only make sense as the solicitousness of a lover. The two editors included an epilogue in which they offered historical context, cited relevant historiography including Gad Beck's memoir – but said nothing of the fact that Aviram was Beck's lover.[98] I asked the editors why they chose to silence this important aspect. Beate Kosmala, who since has familiarized herself with the queer history of the Nazi persecution, having translated Joanna Ostrowska's important study of persecuted Polish queer men during the Nazi occupation, wrote to me that back then, she did not want to challenge Aviram. Today, she would do things differently.[99]

As sunny as Beck's narration is, his memoir has dark sides. Alongside the constant danger of arrest, torture, and deportation to Auschwitz, the fate that some of his closest and dearest met, Beck often brings up sexual violence. He does that directly, while always stressing his agency. Readers often express unease with how nonchalant Beck is in describing various hierarchical sexual encounters and relationships.[100] This trend starts with his first sexual experiences, with adult men who had the duty of care towards him as a child: first with the husband of his aunt at the age of nine and then his first sexual act with a PE teacher at twelve years of age. Beck depicted both encounters as wholly positive. At fifteen, Beck had to leave school when his parents were no longer able to afford to pay his fees and started working, first at a tailor shop and later in a cardboard factory. One of his colleagues here assaulted women workers and sometimes also Beck.[101] In summer 1944, Beck started sleeping with his boss at his forced labour assignment, Richard Wählisch, who offered help with putting up Jews in hiding in exchange for sex. Beck went to some length to explain that he enjoyed these intimacies and was attracted to Wählisch, who held up his part of the deal and offered good care to those in hiding.

An even more troubling arrangement started just before, when Beck met Paul Dreyer, an engineer at a chemistry company. Dreyer offered him an apartment to go into hiding on the condition that he could visit regularly and have sex with Beck. Beck noted that Dreyer was handsome but he was not attracted to him nor did he like the sex. Beck also described an even more exploitative situation: Dreyer offered the use of the shower in his apartment to the Ukrainian forced labourers in his factory in exchange for sex. Another instance of sexual violence remained unmentioned: Beck tells us about a young Jewish man, whom Dreyer supported in hiding and who was his "lover." Eventually, the young man was able to escape to Switzerland and Dreyer missed him dearly.[102] Martina Voigt drew my attention to the fact that the story behind this short sketch is far uglier: the young man was still a teenager for whom the encounters with his rescuer were sexual violence. The man was traumatized for the rest of his life and never had the strength to share his story.[103] Dreyer himself became subjected to sexual violence in the final months of the war: the Gestapo arrested him, deported him to Sachsenhausen as a prisoner with pink triangle, where he was tortured and lost his ears and genitals.

Was Schwersenz's relationship with the teenagers and young men sexual abuse, too? Beck makes it clear that he kept his distance from Schwersenz, not only because he found him too dogmatic but also because he disapproved of Schwersenz's sexual interest in boys. In fact, Beck himself was warned when he first met Schwersenz. Schwersenz was particularly close to Leopold Chones, a Berlin orphan born in 1924 who had been part of his scouting group since 1938. Chones was made to leave in 1941 because of a supposed misstep and rejoined in 1943. The Gestapo captured Chones in October 1943 and tortured him. Chones managed to send out a letter to Schwersenz: "I have fought and remained silent ... Oh, you, my dear one [mein Lieber], do not worry about me. Save yourselves. I will stay brave and strong. We will meet again, so the Lord wants. But I thank you for all that you have given me."[104] In his interview with Lutz van Dijk, Schwersenz described the relationship as love and shared a letter from Chones that he wrote just before his arrest. Here, Chones stated that he reciprocated Schwersenz's romantic feelings.[105] Schwersenz cited from this letter in his memoir but removed this particular section.[106] By the time the two expressed their feelings, Chones was nineteen years of age. He was nine years younger than Schwersenz, and both of them still saw each other as pupil and teacher.[107] Schwersenz was always attracted to "much younger men," as he told van Dijk.[108] How much younger – and what he did with them – he did not elucidate. He must have known that such an admission could damage his reputation as a teacher, which is probably why he demanded those changes in Beck's memoir.

To answer the question: I do not think the relationship was abusive. Nevertheless, it strikes me as problematic. That, however, applies to many other queer wartime relationships that Gad Beck described. Here lies the real job of a historian: to examine how people understood and made sense of their relationships and sexuality in general. Beck's nonchalant narrative of sexual encounters as a child with grown men who were in position of authority needs to be read not only with our sense of deep discomfort; it also allows us to historicize how people in the 1930s and 1940s understood sex with minors, namely in a much less serious light than we do today.[109] In addition, Beck recognized sex and affection as a commodity that he, a charming and winsome young man, could barter.[110] He also chose to narrate these often coercive encounters as matters that **he chose** to endure, found humorous, could navigate and trick, and in some instances, found enjoyable. Did these events really play out like this, or did Beck seek to have ex post facto narrative agency?

We should also bear in mind that Beck's decision to engage in sexual barter was his chosen means to save people. These exchanges served, alongside his immense organizational skills and charisma, to lead a resistance group that successfully saved the lives of dozens of people. The filmmakers of *The Story of Gad Beck* asked Beck whether what he described as "bad sex" was not really rape. He responded: "If I would have seen homosexuality in such a tragic light as you two do, or others, too, I would have hanged myself a long time ago!!"[111] Possibly, whether a coercive sexual barter is something to be endured or a moment of trauma depends on one's age, sexual orientation, sexual drive, and, most importantly, personality. Beck was able to laugh about Dreyer; his predecessor, the boy who escaped to Switzerland, remained scarred. Beck's way of framing his experience was that of an active fighter; he refused the role of a victim. At a public event in February 2000 with Pierre Seel, a

French queer survivor of torture and concentration camps, Beck was visibly uneasy.[112]

Finally, the example of Chug Chaluzi demonstrates how little the category "homosexuality" helps to explain. Even though two of the surviving members, and both its leaders, identified as gay (one in the closet, the second one openly), the sexual and romantic relationships they had with a number of other male members cannot be described as "homosexual." Not only did these men never identify as gay, they have also, if they bore testimony, gone to some lengths to distance themselves from Beck and "his" homosexuality. The concept of "queer acts and practices," as experience and part of the habitus that tied the group together, offers instead a suitable way to understand the group and their bonds. Beck was not aware of the notion of queerness, and operated in his memoir on the binary of "gay/not gay." He was also attracted to heterosexual-identified men, whom he actively sought out and seduced. But to understand these desires and sexual acts, the notion of sexual identity is not helpful. Is it instead queerness as an umbrella category?

Queer Desire in Theresienstadt

How can we write a queer Holocaust history against this backdrop of homophobia and erased sources? I offer a solution in the following section while discussing queer desire and homophobia in Theresienstadt. Two reasons explain the focus on this ghetto. I am acquainted with its history and sources in great detail, having written a book and dozens of articles.[113] Given the fragmentary and hidden nature of queer sources in the Holocaust, this detailed knowledge was necessary to allow me to discern the queer stories. Second, because Theresienstadt was, like all ghettos, a mixed-sex camp, it allows us to observe the degree to which queer desire was a statement on the subjective position of the protagonists rather than the simple absence of heterosexual intimate opportunities, which was the case in most of the concentration camps that were monosexual.

Egon (Gonda) Redlich was a young Zionist from Olomouc, Czechoslovakia. In Theresienstadt, where the SS ordered the Jewish self-administration to oversee much of the day-to-day organization, he headed the Youth Care Department alongside Fredy Hirsch. This department supervised the lives of the children in the ghetto, most of whom were accommodated in youth homes, a more advantageous accommodation. Redlich's diary is one of the best-known Jewish journals from the Holocaust. On 10 September 1944, Redlich remarked: "Two female youth workers worked together. One loves the other with pathological love. I was forced to let her go."[114] Redlich did not characterize his queer colleague as a bad worker; in his depiction, she was deviant because of what he called "pathological" love for another woman. His dismissal of the other youth care worker was homophobically motivated.

On 15 June 1943, Redlich wrote about two teenage girls in love in a youth home. This entry included a similarly awkward formulation that shifted between suggesting two girls in love and one singled out as a problem. He described one girl loving the other with exaggerated love and one of the girls attempting suicide.[115] Because the girls from his 1943 diary were not his staff but rather his charges, Redlich could not fire them. Still, his homophobic attitude influenced the fact that he found them noteworthy and presented their relationship as a problem.

This evidence of the sacked queer youth care worker captured in Redlich's homophobic commentary was further erased when it was not printed in the Hebrew publication of Redlich's diary, edited by Ruth Bondy, the doyenne of Israeli Terezín historiography.[116] Because the English edition of Redlich's diary was based on the Hebrew one and was not compared with the original, it unfortunately features the same omissions. We thus have a double erasure at hand: first when the woman was sacked from the Youth Care Department, the second when the very evidence of her removal was itself removed from the historical record. Sixteen years later, writing for an anthology that became a key text for the study of women and the Holocaust, Bondy argued that queer desire among women was not a part of the Theresienstadt ghetto. She wrote, "Lesbian relationships were extremely rare in the ghetto; most of the young women of my age, including me, had been brought up in puritanical homes and did not even know what the word lesbian meant."[117] Bondy's censorship of same-sex traces indicates that queerness, rather than being rare, was something she was indeed aware of but wished had not appeared. I have not been able to identify these queer youth care workers from Redlich's diary.

The firing of the unnamed queer woman was repeated in March 1945 in the epidemics unit of the Theresienstadt hospital. The young Danish Jew Ralph Oppenhejm noted about his friend, a nurse who worked there: "I have not seen Marianne. Poor thing, she is thrown out from the hospital because she had [sexual] relations one night with a woman in there. A patient passed by and saw it, and surprise, surprise. – yes yes, it does not come as a surprise to me."[118] Oppenhejm's final sentence attests to the fact that he was an out gay man. The inmates in proximity to Oppenhejm knew about his sexuality. His diary represents the only journal by a queer protagonist that we have for Theresienstadt. In fact, Oppenhejm's diary is to my knowledge the only journal by a queer Jew written during the Holocaust. Deported with his family to Theresienstadt in October 1943, Oppenhejm was perceived as charming and amusing. But in light of his diary, it seems that he spent a significant amount of time and energy ingratiating himself to his mostly female friends to come across as likable.[119] Scholars such as Laurie Marhoefer have pointed out how crucial social capital was for the safety of queer people in Nazi Germany.[120] The other factor contributing to his social acceptance by others was the fact that while in the ghetto, it appears that Oppenhejm was not sexually active, as far as we can conclude from his diary and the recollections of his sister Ellen.[121] The sacked nurse too remained nameless: I was not able to identify Marianne.[122] None of the former nurses who are still alive remembered her. There were at least thirty women of that age and first name at that point in Theresienstadt.

Susanne Fall was a young woman from Ostrava who worked for the Transport Help unit assisting the arriving transports. Shortly after liberation, Fall wrote a blunt report about her time in Theresienstadt in which she described her experiences as part of the Theresienstadt social elite. While in the ghetto, Fall had her first sexually intimate experience, with a man. Discovering her sexuality was for her a source of pleasure. For younger people, sexuality was an important way of coming to terms with imprisonment.[123] In November 1943, Fall aided older prisoners who were categorized as "prominent":

> At this occasion I am also to announce the return of a patient (an old prominent lady who has a room of her own in the Magdeburg barrack). I have to knock at the door for a long time. I hear aroused whispering and when the door is opened, I see a tousled bed, 2 women with morning gowns hastily thrown over, visibly embarrassed and aroused. A terrible disgust comes over me, I never knew that such a thing is possible even here.[124]

Why was it that Fall, who started to be sexually active only a few weeks earlier and described the beginning of her intimate life as beautiful and meaningful, reacted with "terrible disgust" when encountering same-sex desire? In contrast to Bondy's statement, Fall was aware of the existence of queer desire. Like Bondy, she wished that Theresienstadt would be free of it. As for the identity of the woman, again, we can only speculate. The term "prominent" described a category of prisoners with additional privileges deriving from their pre-deportation status who received better accommodation and food.[125] A room of their own, as the woman above had, was a rare privilege, while ordinary inmates shared crowded accommodation; most prominent prisoners had a double room occupancy. One obvious candidate for the woman Fall remembered would be Martha Mosse, the first police councillor (Polizeirätin) for the Prussian police and later a functionary of the Reich Association of Jews in Germany. We know that Mosse had lived in Berlin with a gentile female partner, was deported alone, and in Theresienstadt was a "prominent" prisoner.[126] But we will never know for certain, as there were several older single prominent women in Theresienstadt. What is important here is the pattern of the structural anonymity of these women, whose seemingly consensual sexual activity was perceived in their social setting with disgust.

The last two cases show how two openly queer persons, Fredy Hirsch and Harry "Hambo" Heyman, navigated the prisoner society in Theresienstadt that tolerated them – up to a point. Fredy Hirsch was born in 1916 in Aachen and grew up without a father. As a teenager he was already active in the Zionist movement, which was the reason why he did not accompany his remarried mother and brother when they emigrated to Bolivia in the 1930s. In 1934, at seventeen years of age, Hirsch relocated to Frankfurt am Main where he led a group of about fifteen boys and girls within the Jewish Scouts League. From this time we have the first mentions of Hirsch's queerness, coded negatively: the boys felt that Hirsch approached them too intimately.[127] Later, he worked for Maccabi, a Zionist youth organization, in Dresden. Following a skirmish with the stormtroopers, he had to leave Germany.[128] In 1936, Hirsch emigrated to Czechoslovakia and eventually settled down

Figure 1.5. Photo of Fredy Hirsch from the late 1930s.
Source: Courtesy of Beit Theresienstadt.

in Brno, the largest city in Moravia, with a mixed German- and Czech-speaking population.[129] In Brno, he worked for the local branch of Maccabi, a Zionist organization, and ran the sports and summertime activities for children and teenagers. He was paid reasonably well, one thousand crowns per month. Hirsch proved to be excellent at working with children, motivating them for hikes, telling stories, while teaching them discipline. The children and adults alike were impressed with his good athletic looks and direct personality. In particular when he negotiated with Germans, he never kowtowed nor showed fear, greatly impressing the survivors and apparently also the perpetrators. In 1939, after the Nazi occupation, he moved to Prague and continued working in the youth movement.

This experience, together with his work helping organize the emigration of the Zionist youth to Denmark, helped Fredy foster close connections with key leaders of the Czech Zionists. In fall 1941, the SS decided to send all Czech Jews to Theresienstadt and ordered the Zionist leadership in the occupied Protectorate of Bohemia and Moravia to function as a Jewish Council. Hirsch was part of the transport Stab that carried the twenty-four closest colleagues of the first Elder of the Jews, Jakob Edelstein. In the ghetto, Hirsch headed the Youth Care Department together with Gonda Redlich. Youth Care established youth homes for young people under the age of eighteen. This separate accommodation offered many advantages to children: first, their parents had to work like all adult prisoners and thus could not take care of their children. The youth homes, which were separated according to age, language, and sex, were less overcrowded than the overall accommodation. Children also received better and more nutritious food rations, while most youth care workers sincerely worked hard to give the best possible care and, as far as it was possible, education.

In Theresienstadt, Hirsch became the idol of the teenage children he supervised. With his sports activities, team spirit, and insistence on discipline, he succeeded in creating a relatively happy and safe world for the children inside the terrifying and dirty place.[130] Since teenagers, unlike young children, had a better chance of survival and thus could bear testimony after the war, Hirsch has been singled out for celebration far more than most of his colleagues.[131] In September 1943, Hirsch was among the five thousand Jews deported to the Theresienstadt Family Camp in Auschwitz.

The Family Camp was a subsection of Birkenau in existence between September 1943 and July 1944; here, the SS held men and women, children, adults, and the elderly alike. In these dreary conditions, Hirsch succeeded in organizing effective care for children in two separate barracks. On 8 March, 1944, the SS murdered nearly all people from the September transport and with them also Hirsch. To this date, historians disagree on the circumstances of his death: whether he committed suicide, accidentally overdosed with tranquilizers, or was killed. Some see his potential suicide as a proof of the weakness of character of a gay man.[132] Having studied all the materials, my opinion is that we cannot ascertain how Hirsch died. We know, though, that he died at twenty-eight years of age, victim of the Nazis.

People in Terezín knew that Hirsch was gay. We do not know how he understood and communicated his sexuality, not least since only fragments of his extensive correspondence survive.[133] But I think we can speculate that he identified as a gay man: in Brno he lived with his partner, the Czech-speaking medical student Jan Mautner.[134] Mautner's niece as well as the niece of Mautner's postwar partner, Walter Löwy, knew that their uncles were gay. Hirsch's gayness was well known and seemingly accepted by the fellow prisoners. There are even stories of a young woman who fell in love with the good-looking Fredy and was hugely upset when she learned that as a gay man, he would not reciprocate. Significantly, her reaction was disappointment, not disgust.[135]

When we look more closely, though, the tolerance wears thin. Children would make fun of Hirsch's accent and effeminate ways.[136] Jan Mautner has almost effectively disappeared from the public record. What did survive, though, were rumours that Hirsch was sexually attracted to boys. Whispers of "less honorable motivations for escape [to Czechoslovakia]" supposedly accompanied Hirsch at his arrival in Czechoslovakia in 1935.[137] Adults would warn boys never to stay with Hirsch alone in the room.[138] Several survivors recalled that when they were with Hirsch alone in the evening, they felt uncomfortable.[139] Tomáš Fantl, at that point twelve or thirteen years old, remembered that before the deportation, Hirsch put his hand into the boy's underpants. After that, the boy's older brother beat Hirsch up.[140] It is disappointing that almost none of the many works on Hirsch address these accusations of pedophilia.[141] There is a logic to the rumours: Dotan Brom has called this situation the "transparent closet." Gossip is a particular manner of conveying information since it serves as a form of policing. The gossip ensured that Hirsch's queerness could not be a legitimate fact that he could own; instead, it was one that was only the stuff of rumours that made him the sexual other.[142]

Why was Hirsch's sexuality, and by extension molestation of children, not accepted, as was the case for Jizchak Schwersenz, at least if we can believe Gad Beck's storytelling? There were two factors at play. First, Chug Chaluzi operated largely as a group of young people without parents and also, since many of its members were in hiding, offered the only meaningful opportunity to socialize. The young men and teenagers around Schwersenz thus did not have many people around them to express doubts to or to start gossiping with. However, Schwersenz led a group of admiring Jewish teenagers since the late 1930s, when they very much had parents and a social setting that could have offered pushback. Here, a second factor played a role: like Schwersenz, Hirsch was charismatic and good-looking, but unlike him, he was a foreigner who never spoke Czech well. In Theresienstadt, ethnicity became a defining category of belonging, while Czech Jews, the largest group in the ghetto, depicted German and other prisoners as irritatingly different.[143] This intersectional identity as queer **and** a foreigner marked Hirsch as other, which is why people were less willing to accept his sexuality (and especially his sexual abuse).

The eyewitness testimony of Tomáš Fantl is a serious reminder that we need to engage with this difficult history. For a long time, in fact until now, scholarship and commemoration of gay men persecuted by the Nazis skirted, or even concealed, the fact that some of them had been sentenced not only for sex with adult men but also with boys.[144] Part of the problem of why the sexual abuse of children was neglected for so long is that parts of the male youth movement in Germany tolerated (in some cases even propagated) sexual abuse of children and teenagers.[145] Molestation of children was a crime that in the first half of the twentieth century could be used to depict the perpetrator as particularly deviant, but at the same time could be trivialized. It is entirely possible that Hirsch was all these things: a brave man who inspired imprisoned Jewish youth, gave them meaning and motivation in their last months; a boyfriend of a tall, handsome Moravian physician; and a man who sometimes molested some of the boys in his care.

The position of the clown and female impersonator Hambo is one last example of a queer and possibly gender non-conforming person. I do not know whether Hambo self-identified as gender non-conforming. In the surviving sources, Hambo speaks of themself using masculine pronouns. I chose to use the pronoun "they" for Hambo and discuss them as a trans character, not to apply identity markers but, as Susan Stryker suggested, to leave space for not knowing.[146] I include them here to offer an example of how a trans biography in the Holocaust could have looked.[147]

Hambo's complexity disturbed the increasingly rigid sexual and gender categories in which the victim society operated. As Rainer Herrn points out, some female impersonators self-identified as heterosexual. But those who had sex with men could be persecuted, castrated, and sent to concentration camps.[148] Recent research by Laurie Marhoefer and Bodie Ashton has demonstrated that the Nazi state was aware of and persecuted trans people for their transness, their very being gender non-conforming.[149]

Who were female impersonators? In a way, we can see them as ancestors to drag artists today. They were men employed in a recognized profession, in which they put on women's clothes in the context of a performance, as Jacob Bloomfield's helpful definition states.[150] The performance could be funny, sexually suggestive, surprising in terms of the perfection of passing, or awe-inducing as a comment on gender norms. Scholars such as Susan Stryker and Jacob Bloomfield include female impersonation and drag as a form of gender variance and trans history.[151] Female impersonators could also be seen in the context of transvestitism in the sense of habitual cross-dressing, such as for sexual arousal. We also need to bear in mind that the German term "Transvestit" in the period 1900 to around 1950 would approximately translate to our understanding of trans* or transgender today.[152] Some of the female impersonators were straight men, some were queer, and some were people whom today we would understand as trans.

Harry "Hambo" Heymann, born in Berlin in 1907, was lucky to escape that fate. They grew up in a middle-class Jewish family and trained as an opera singer at the University for Music (Hochschule für Musik). After their education, they started working as a clown under the nickname "Hambo," specializing as a female impersonator.[153] Attacked by stormtroopers in 1933, they escaped via Stettin, Germany (today Szczecin, Poland), to Helsinki, Finland, and in 1934, went from there to Denmark.[154] They worked as a member of the Cavallini clown group, toured Europe and America, and worked at the Tivoli amusement park in Copenhagen. In October 1943 Hambo was among the almost five hundred Jews in Denmark captured by the Nazis and deported to Theresienstadt.[155] In the ghetto, Hambo became a fixture of cultural life, working as comedian, clown, and female impersonator.

Unlike Fredy Hirsch and Ralph Oppenhejm, Hambo was no longer young and beautiful. They were thirty-seven years old and very thin; in fact, emaciated. Oppenhejm mentioned his fellow gay inmate a few times in his diary, often in cruel terms: "With mother in the café house, where we were invited by [Peter] Deutsch, who directed the orchestra. Met Hambo, who entertained us, much thinner, more sharp in his face, whatever can have caused that (according to the hearsay, he fornicates his soul out of his body).

Figure 1.6. Drawing by Erich Lichtblau, "Hambo, the Pop-Hit Singer."
Source: Image courtesy of Holocaust Museum LA.

He however got more to eat more than most other people, a part earned by his performing, and a part he probably earned by lying down. How the fuck is this possible with this measly appearance, little one?"[156]

Oppenhejm speculated that Hambo earned extra food through sex work, indicating that there was a market for queer male prostitution. But it is possible that Oppenhejm's remark was simply nasty instead of informative; Oppenhejm liked to gossip and be mean. Hambo was also placed in the context of other forms of transgressive sexuality. Like Hirsch, Hambo was rumoured to be attracted to boys. In a short story from 1958, the writer Arnošt Lustig, who as a teenager was imprisoned at Theresienstadt, described a Dutch singer "Hannibal de Hambo." The singer would stroll through the ghetto and "jotted down the names of boys in his [sic] notebooks, inviting the best looking ones into his [sic] room."[157] While Lustig was not a reliable narrator, several Danish survivors recalled that Hambo would "make passes" at boys and young men.[158] There are, however, no testimonies that they harassed anyone physically.

Erich Lichtblau's wartime sketch "Hambo, the Pop-Hit Singer" cements Hambo's othering as a deviant. The artwork, drawn once in 1943 and redrawn in the 1970s, speaks poignantly to Hambo's campness in that it shows their red lips and false eyelashes.[159] Their falsetto voice is alluded to in the rising notes. But all this is shown in combination with signs of an aging, visibly Jewish "man." The receding hairline, wrinkles, glasses, and aquiline nose together radiate a homophobic message. To the viewer, Hambo does not come across as congenial nor do they appear funny by their actions. Hambo's figure is surrounded by ten heads of laughing men. One of the men is pointing his finger at Hambo as an object of laughter: we laugh about them, not with them, because they appear as a shrill and tacky aging drag queen.

Hambo was "lucky" and survived in Theresienstadt. Together with most Danish deportees, at the end of the war they were released to Sweden, where they were reunited with their father. Both their sisters perished during the Holocaust. After the war, Hambo lived again in Denmark. Unfortunately, they were no longer able to perform on stage because of the lasting physical and mental health difficulties from their incarceration. They married a waitress named Edith Jensen. Their friend, a fellow Theresienstadt survivor who was also of German-Jewish background, Leo Säbel, remembered that it was a marriage of convenience and that Edith supported her spouse.[160] Hambo spent their last years in Farum, where they died in 1995. Today, no one remembers them. In 2018, I published a short search article about Hambo in a large Danish newspaper, but there were no responses.[161]

Conclusion

Bearing witness, formulating the historical self, was immensely important for Holocaust survivors. To tell one's own story, to testify, is an elementary part of what I term "historical citizenship." What is of value is not only participation in the emergence of historical narratives but also in becoming visible as a citizen of history, that is, being part of history. Other forms of historical citizenship might be holding on to a name, a grave, or a memorial. This is why those who survived sought to commemorate their dead families and friends with *yizkor bikher* and memorial books, as they held names and stories of the murdered victims who were not able to have a grave.

People without history are dust. Those whose testimony has been made structurally impossible are treated as being without value. The narrator of a life story in our culture must always be virtuous or must repent to become virtuous. A sinner who did not repent, the other constructed as deviant monster, is a priori sinful, and therefore can never tell their story. A person who has been categorized as deviant from the start cannot in this logic have a voice. Since the victim society marked queer victims as deviant, they are barred from being able to tell their whole story. This perspective has shaped Holocaust archives and their politics of collecting, including the decisions about what ought to be collected and what ought not. As historians we work with those sources that exist, directly imprinting on what could be remembered, told, collected, and eventually written as suitable history. The sources that exist shape our own identity, our values, and our judgments.

Emanuel Ringelblum, the great Jewish historian and archivist of the Warsaw ghetto, raised the existential question "Who will write our history?"[162] The queer Holocaust victims have become objects of what Gayatri Spivak has called "epistemic violence."[163] They are not able to bear witness, they are not able to have a voice, and they have been prevented from leaving behind a trace of their own choice in history. They are people without historical citizenship.

What can we take away from this analysis of erasure in order to write a queer history of the Holocaust? First is the necessity of an archaeological approach. This method allows us to deconstruct and analyse the homophobic stories that often represent the point of departure and which can lead us to traces of the real people emerging from these statements. The resulting studies can recuperate the persons from the homophobic anecdotes. The consequent history will likely still have gaps, but it will offer a narrative more inclusive than the heteronormative master narrative of Holocaust survivors. Stories such as the nameless youth care workers, sacked, like the nurse Marianne, for loving and having sex, can start giving us an idea of lived queer lives in the shadow of the Holocaust. Fredy Hirsch and Hambo, two queer German emigrants, were people who inspired and gave hope through sports, pedagogy, and performances in a ghetto. Their ambivalence, the fact that they were sexually attracted to young men and boys, is a reminder of the fact that we need to face queer history with its difficulties, and not to romanticize it or sweep things under the rug.

Embracing these gaps and those people with "failed" biographies offers a prime example of what queer history stands for: it offers a powerful critical lens, questions normativity, and exposes assumptions and arrangements that are taken for granted.[164] Queer history can thus lead to welcoming the inherent messiness and difficulty of the social and sexual hierarchies in the Holocaust victim society. Queer history of the Holocaust questions the assumption of a specific way of being a man or a woman, the romantic and idealized heterosexual love stories at the barbed wire, and in fact the entire redemptive framework of the Shoah. Such a history is not a happy one and does not serve the emancipatory narrative of gay liberation, which might be the reason why gay and lesbian historians have avoided the Holocaust. My research reveals the protagonists as often deeply ambivalent characters, deeply affected by the camps and Nazi persecution. But rather than a statement on queerness per se, their ambivalence needs to be interpreted in the context of the victim society. Including the queer perspective changes the monolithic normative history; it helps us to understand how prescriptive it is in the first place. We will rarely be able to completely unearth the voices of those deemed "unworthy victims" and to change the Holocaust archives entirely. But thinking about the marginalized can help us to develop a less judgmental, more inclusive past.

CHAPTER TWO

People without History Are Dust

In New York in the late 1970s, a woman sat at the table of lesbian historian Joan Nestle. In the years prior, Nestle had founded the *Lesbian Herstory Archive*, which for the first twenty-odd years of its existence was held in her home in New York's Upper West Side. The older visitor noted that Nestle, like herself, was Jewish and explained to Nestle: "I had a chance to read a copy of *The Well of Loneliness* that had been translated into Polish before I was taken into the camps. I was a young girl at the time, around twelve or thirteen, and one of the ways I survived in the camp was by remembering that book. I wanted to live long enough to kiss a woman."[1] *The Well of Loneliness* was a 1928 novel by the British author Radclyffe Hall that thematized the legitimacy of lesbian desire and gender non-conforming identities.[2] In the following years, Nestle shared this poignant anecdote multiple times, including in her review of several Jewish lesbian-feminist publications, *Into the Mainstream*. The voices of queer Holocaust survivors, however, are certainly the opposite of mainstream. Nestle's anecdote about *The Well of Loneliness* has not been recognized at all in Holocaust studies. Hardly any other topic is so silenced, marginalized, and even made taboo as is queer Holocaust history.

This chapter seeks to make up for this loss. I show that queer Holocaust history is not a matter of only a footnote to the Holocaust, but rather how much we learn about central aspects of the Shoah history by uncovering its marginalized features. These include the agency of Holocaust victims, different and varying family structures, prejudices within the camps' prisoner society, or the departure from simple historical linearity. For example, Paulina Pająk has pointed out how Poland decriminalized homosexuality in 1932, long before Great Britain, Germany, or Czechoslovakia. Even before this, the intellectual circle of the publishing house Rój had planned the publication of a Polish translation of *The Well of Loneliness*.[3] The 1933 *Źródło samotności* was well received and spoken of in key literary journals. Far more than just a fascinating anecdote, this history of the Polish translation and publication of the first great lesbian novel shows that a seamless continuity of an illiberal, unprogressive, homophobic, and hyper-Catholic Poland cannot be assumed.[4] Similarly, the argument that there has not yet been an engagement with homosexuality during the Holocaust because people at the time were more homophobic is both ahistorical and too simplistic. Sexuality has a history, and as we examine that history set against our normative

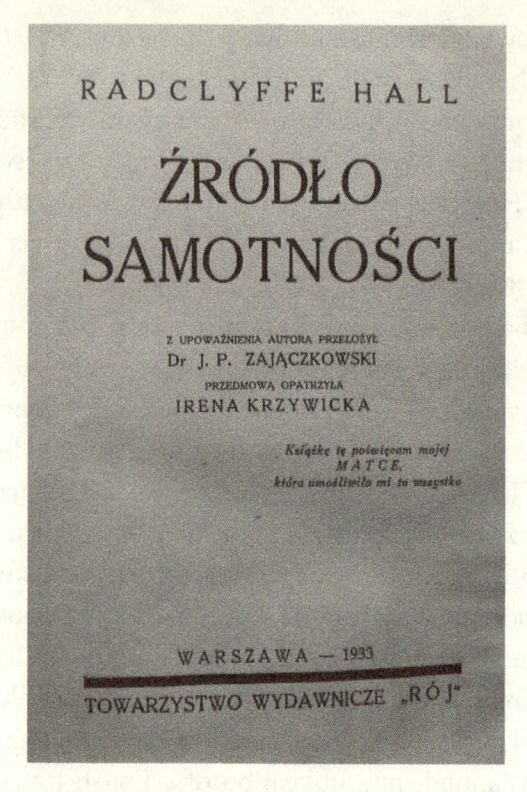

Figure 2.1. Front page of the 1933 Polish edition of *The Well of Loneliness*, *Źródło samotności*, by Radclyffe Hall.

expectations, we shine new light onto topics previously held as true and known.[5]

This chapter offers a queer history of the Holocaust through five case studies of young people. This eponymous chapter 2 of *People without History Are Dust* focuses on teenagers, foremost because the source pool for adolescents is somewhat larger, but above all because I wish to reveal how five youths who gave their testimonies at different times – three girls and two boys; two born in Poland, two in Germany, and one in what is today the Czech Republic – recall queerness. I consider how sexual encounters and relations inside the camps were defined by dependency and exploitation. I illustrate how a queer reading of the Holocaust enables the recognition of the new forms of family and kinship that arose during and after deportation, forced separation, and murder of family relations and that are manifested through expressions of loss and the memories of survivors, which is, furthermore, why we should take these forms of kinship seriously.[6] Throughout, the chapter focuses on the themes of powerlessness and agency of Holocaust victims and demonstrates how the lens of sexuality helps to capture significant insights in this regard. This is particularly important here because such focus takes seriously the decision-making possibilities of Holocaust victims, something other scholars have often failed to adequately acknowledge following Lawrence Langer's argument of "choiceless choices."[7]

Queer history is all too often a history of men. It is no accident that Robert Beachy's celebrated study *Gay Berlin* is above all concerned with male homosexuality.[8] Although queer Holocaust history has been almost completely suppressed, four prominent memoirs from Holocaust survivors identifying as either lesbian or gay exist, three from men and one from a woman.[9] In order to bring attention to more female voices, in the following pages I predominantly focus on stories from women.

The examples in this chapter complicate simple categorizations of lesbian or gay, which is why I use the concept "queer" as an umbrella term. Crucial to this conceptual shift is Jennifer Evans's warning to remain aware of the danger in assuming a rigid sexual identity which then conceals our view of the fragmented and ambivalent nature of these "acts and practices."[10] Moreover, queer history's methodological practices claim to scrutinize and question the accustomed, normative frames of historical reference. These norms are substantial and often exclusionary, especially in the case of Holocaust history. Scholars have debated the emergence of distinct sexual subjectivities, and this chapter offers significant insights to this history.

When a reader today for the first time notices that they fancy someone of the same sex, the chances are they will start thinking about what it means for their sexual orientation. This subjectivity, I must stress as a historian, is entirely modern. Robert Beachy has put the date of German men and women starting to self-define as "homosexual" into the early 1900s; the same took much longer in Britain, suggests Laura Doan.[11] This chapter shows how young people in the Nazi camps and ghettos started becoming aware of their sexual identity. Margot Heuman knew she was attracted to women, and learned in fall 1944 from prisoners gossiping about a lesbian guard that this meant a distinct sexual identity. Melania Weissenberg came to the ghetto with the knowledge of lesbian love at the age of eleven, and debated in her diary how to tell the woman she loved not only of her feelings but also of what they meant in terms of subjectivity. Nate Leipciger endured queer sexual violence and violent sexual barter; after the liberation, he sought out heterosexual intimacy to confirm his heterosexuality. Finally, Jiří Vrba shows us a model of self-determined gay life in a state and family that did not welcome this decision, and yet Vrba made his way.

The chapter is divided into six parts: one section on queer theory and five case examples. First, I examine the life history of Margot Heuman. Her biography leads to an investigation of queer kinship, or the possibilities of so-called non-biological family configurations, which emerged during the Holocaust. The next four life histories are of Nate Leipciger, a victim of sexual abuse who nevertheless spoke of his abuser's "affection," followed by an exploration of the diaries of two young women in hiding that are commonly read as heterosexual: Anne Frank and Molly Applebaum. I reveal how through a queer interpretation of these texts we can uncover traces of same-sex love within them. The essay closes with the story of the Czech Holocaust survivor Jiří Vrba, who contributed to the appreciation of the cultural life of Theresienstadt but as a gay man became almost entirely forgotten.

Margot Heuman

Margot Heuman was the first lesbian survivor deported as a Jew who gave testimony and spoke about her queerness. I first came across Heuman in 2017 when her relative contacted me after hearing of my research. I had designed my work as public history, guessing that my best chance to find sources would be if I presented my work outside of academic circles as well. That gamble paid off when Linda Heuman contacted me six months after a talk at Hebrew

University. Linda, who is herself queer, had visited her father's cousin, Margot, in Arizona. During that visit, Margot came out to Linda.

Margot was born in 1928, the eldest daughter of retailer Karl Heumann and his wife Johanna, in Hellenthal, in the Eifel mountain range near the Belgian border.[12] (After she emigrated to the US, she dropped one "n" from her last name, becoming "Heuman.") Three years later, her younger sister Lore was born. The girls spent a happy childhood in the Eifel and later in the then Free State of Lippe. The family was economically successful, and Margot had many relatives with whom to play. In 1937 the Heumanns moved to Bielefeld (Lippe) where her father worked for the Hilfsverein der Juden in Deutschland (Relief organization of German Jews). Already as a child, Margot was aware of her attraction towards other girls; early in our conversations, she recalled her best friend, who after starting puberty would wear a tight sweater with a breast pocket. Margot explained with a laugh, "I used to tell her that I loved her pocket and could I put my hand in her pocket." To my follow-up question about this friend, Margot answered, "She was not lesbian. She married, and as far as I know she had no further relationships with women."[13] A recurring motif throughout Heuman's account, her response to my question on the intensity of the relationship was "We never spoke about it."

From September 1941, like all Jews in Greater Germany, Margot and her family had to wear the yellow star; shortly thereafter the deportations began. Because her father then worked for the District Office of the Hilfsverein, the Heumanns were not deported to Riga and Auschwitz in 1942

Figure 2.2. Photo of Margot Heuman from 1946.
Source: Courtesy of the family of Margot Heuman.

like most of Bielefeld's Jews; rather, in June 1943 they were sent to the Theresienstadt ghetto.[14] Karl Heumann worked in the post office.

In Theresienstadt, children had the opportunity to live in youth homes, which were less overcrowded accommodations where children received slightly more substantial food.[15] Because prisoners had to work, youth homes also offered a solution to child supervision. Margot noticed that difference between her experience of Theresienstadt and that of her parents: "My life was so different from theirs." Children were separated by gender, age, and language, and thus Margot and her sister were placed in two different homes. Margot was placed in a home based in L414, run by Anka Lenkawitzová. Today, visitors to the town of Terezín look at the building as they wait for the public transport bus back to Prague.[16] Like most other youth homes in

Theresienstadt, the girls were raised as Zionists; after the liberation, Margot was considering going to Palestine.[17] The teenagers were sometimes sent to help in the agriculture section, where Margot would steal spinach and bring it to her parents to improve their rations. Interviewing Margot, I realized that her youth care worker, Anka Lenkawitzová, was the same woman who, at the end of the war, escaped from a death march, made her way to Prague, and hid with my paternal great grandparents in their allotment in Prague Hrdlořezy. In 1999, Lenkawitzová arranged for them to be recognized as Righteous among the Nations.[18]

In the youth home, Margot met Edith (Dita) Neumann, a young girl from Vienna, one month younger. Dita was deported to Theresienstadt without her parents, accompanied only by her aunt and grandmother; her mother died when Dita was only six, and her father escaped to England. Margot fell in love with Dita, and the pair were inseparable. At night, they laid in the same bed and held each other. Margot explained to me, "We did not actually have sex. Very close to it, but no sex." By day Margot and Dita were seen as best friends, especially since Dita also had a boyfriend. "I was jealous," Margot recounted, "but there was nothing I could do about it and I didn't. At that time, I was smart enough not to make a big fuss." At fifteen, Margot already knew that her love had no place in public.

Dita and Margot were not the only girls to share a bed at night. Margot recalled that at least one other couple did so. Both girls from this other couple survived, and one of them wrote a memoir. The author recalls how in her youth home, several girls had "best friends," but she mentions neither love nor intimacy.[19] This insight in Margot's account invites questions of how many other queer relationships there may have been but were not spoken about, if not accidentally recalled by someone like Fredy Hirsch or Margot Heuman.

In the ghetto, Margot came to know her other great passion: the opera. Cultural life in Theresienstadt was an important source of support for the prisoners; an importance that is, with good reason, appreciated today, also thanks to the engagement of Jiří Vrba, the protagonist of the last section of this chapter. The first performance Heuman witnessed was Theresienstadt's production of *La Bohème*. Her eyes lit up as she spoke of hearing the aria "Che gelida manina" for the first time: "How cold your little hand is! Let me warm it for you." Decades later, Heuman would become a dedicated visitor to the New York Metropolitan Opera. Opera is, as queer historians have shown, an important aspect of queer and homosexual subculture.[20]

In May 1944, the Heumanns were deported to the Theresienstadt Family Camp in Auschwitz-Birkenau. Here, the prisoners did not have to undergo a selection and thus children, men, women, and the elderly lived together in one camp section. In May 1944, the SS ordered 7,500 people from Theresienstadt onto three transports dispatched to Auschwitz-Birkenau on 15, 16, and 18 May 1944. Margot wept ceaselessly during the deportation because she was separated from Dita. Then, only two days after the Heumanns, Dita and her aunt also arrived. "It was a miracle." Reunited with Dita, Margot was happy – in Auschwitz. She and Dita worked in a barrack where they cared for small children – a continuation of the Jewish self-administration in Theresienstadt. One of their fellow care workers was Jiří Vrba, who was deported in the same deportation wave.

Most of the prisoners in the Family Camp learned of the gas chambers at Birkenau and so too did both girls. Heuman recalled: "We didn't know anything about our future, and I decided that if Dita goes to the gas chamber, then I'm going with her. I never ever have loved anyone the way I loved Dita." The Family Camp was liquidated at the beginning of July 1944.[21] The inhabitants knew what the coming selection meant; those considered capable of work would be selected for forced labour while the rest would be gassed. Dita and her aunt Lisl Spira survived the selection, while her grandmother Klara Radlmesser was sent to the gas. Margot's parents did not even attempt to escape their murder because they saw no chance of protecting Margot's thirteen-year-old sister. Margot, however, decided to follow Dita. Margot's mother was outraged, believing the family should stay together, but as Margot said goodbye to her father, he blessed her. For the first time, she saw him cry. Nevertheless, at the time all her thoughts were of Dita. As she recounted this to me in 2018, she wept. Later, I was able to find out that Margot's mother Johanna, who was then forty-two years old, and Lore, who was thirteen, were sent to Stutthof. Johanna perished on 1 October 1944, while Lore's death date we do not know; possibly she perished, like so many, on the death marches in February 1945.[22] I was able to share this finding with Margot, which gave her a measure of comfort.

In the women's camp in Birkenau, Margot and Dita were placed on transport to a satellite camp of concentration camp Neuengamme in Hamburg.[23] The Jewish women from Auschwitz, six hundred from Theresienstadt and four hundred from Hungary, were the first female prisoners there. Starved and weak, they were forced to dispose of rubble and build emergency accommodation for bombed out civilians, suffering the working days almost always in the open air. Margot's group passed through three camps: Dessauer Ufer in the harbour, Neugraben in the south-west, and Tiefstack in south-east Hamburg. While in the satellite camps, it became apparent the importance that age played in one's camp experience. While the older women suffered from the rough handling of the guards as well as from hunger and cold, the sixteen-year-old girls also experienced the camp as an adventure; in Neugraben they collected mushrooms in the nearby forest and rolled down a hill in freshly fallen snow. To be sure, Dita and Margot were hungry, but they always found a way to scavenge something edible they could share. Dita was Margot's be-all and end-all. The pair also secured a bed at the end of the barrack in which they could be together at night.

Their queer relationship between both girls met with some pushback. At one point Margot heard a loud remark, "That is not normal." Dita's aunt defended them by pointing out that they were both still children. Margot also noticed a coerced relationship between one of the women guards, Anneliese Kohlmann, and a beautiful Jewish woman from Prague. "We knew that she had special privileges," Margot told me. "I know that they were constantly together, and she did it to survive."[24] Some of the older women spoke about Kohlmann, calling her a lesbian. That was the first time Margot, who already knew that women could love women but did not have a word for it, learned this expression and came to understand herself thus.

At the beginning of April 1945, the SS dissolved the satellite camp and sent the women to Bergen-Belsen. The conditions in Hamburg were wretched, but in Bergen-Belsen the terrors were still greater. When the British army liberated the camp on 15 April, Margot was ill with typhus and weighed only thirty-five kilograms. For two months she lay in hospital before being brought to Sweden to recuperate in July. Dita was able to go to England. She trained there as a midwife. Margot spent two years in Sweden where she recovered, learned Swedish, and for the first time was able to lead something of a "normal" teenage life. Although she liked Sweden, she immigrated to the US in 1947 to join relatives. Initially she only intended to stay for a year, but the lesbian life in New York enthralled her.[25] She enjoyed the queer culture of Greenwich Village and moved in with her girlfriend, the legendary *New Yorker* copy editor Lu Burke. Thanks to Burke, Margot's English improved – they went together word by word through a thesaurus. Through another lesbian connection, Margot received a job with Dayle Dayne Bernbach, which in time would become one of the largest advertising agencies in the world.

At the beginning of the 1950s, Heuman decided she wanted children; however, the only way to make this dream a reality, in her eyes, was to marry a man. She separated from Burke and in 1953 married a colleague from another agency. On the surface, the next twenty years of Margot's life appear to be the fulfilment of the quintessential American dream. She gave birth to two children and lived in a house in Brooklyn. Eventually, with the help of Lissy, a Black housekeeper, Margot was able to pursue her career.[26] At the same time, Margot maintained an affair with a woman from her neighbourhood, their husbands believing them to be best friends. In this respect, Margot was part of a much

Figure 2.3. Photo of Margot Heuman and Dita Neumann at Dita's wedding in 1956.
Source: Courtesy of the family of Margot Heuman.

larger American lesbian history.[27] When asked whether or not her husband noticed anything, Heuman stressed, "I am a very good actress." In the 1970s her marriage fell apart. Only at eighty-eight did she chance a fresh start by coming out to her family when she moved to Arizona. The reaction of Heuman's daughter-in-law was indicative; she merely laughed and said, "What else is new?" Her whole family knew that their mother and grandmother was a lesbian, but only now could they speak about it.

Margot was interviewed multiple times for various Holocaust archives. The story which she shared with me was, in its basic components, included in both of the oral history interviews she gave to two important Holocaust archives, the Visual History Archive and the United States Holocaust Memorial Museum. Only the aspect of queer love was left out with Dita appearing only as the "best friend."[28] No one asked why she was so important to Margot. The silencing of Margot's queerness is symptomatic of almost all oral histories with Holocaust survivors.[29]

Since 2010, I have been encouraging the Shoah Foundation to acknowledge and address this erasure, to no avail. Thus, I was surprised when I found out that the Shoah Foundation published a clip of Margot's testimony for queer history month in 2023 as *Surviving Together/Queer Holocaust Survivor Margot Heuman(n)*. The caption stated: "To celebrate the first day of Pride Month, we honor LGBTQ+ survivors of the Holocaust, and recall how difficult living – and speaking – candidly was until recent years."[30] Unfortunately, the caption did not say that it was the structures of testifying for the Shoah Foundation that made it so hard to speak about queerness, nor did the caption acknowledge that it was my work that enabled Margot's testimony, which allowed the Shoah Foundation to recognize the queer undertones in their interview with her. All's well that ends well – and a reminder that some things deserve to be fought for: after my intervention and that of many colleagues, the caption was changed, and I was invited to present my work.[31]

Margot and Dita remained in contact their entire lives. Dita moved to Toronto in the 1950s in order to be closer to Margot in New York and married a physician. The two women saw each other every summer. The never renewed their romantic relationship, and they spoke neither of their connection in the camps nor of Margot's later relationships

Figure 2.4. Photo of Margot Heuman and Anna Hájková in 2018.
Source: Courtesy of the author.

with other women. As Dita lay in her deathbed at eighty-three years old, dying of sudden cancer, she waited until Margot came to her side before passing so that they could say goodbye. Only at this moment did Margot tell Dita that she loved her all her life.

I cherished my friendship with Margot. We met three times, in Arizona in 2018, in Hamburg in 2019, and then in April 2022 in Arizona again. The planned visits in between were disrupted by the pandemic, which was hard on Margot. Margot was vivacious, mischievous, funny, and generous. She commented on my statuses on social media, texted on WhatsApp, and even purchased and read my first book on Theresienstadt. She enjoyed the attention that came with my publications and talks, but occasionally also expressed ambivalence, such as when someone built her a Wikipedia entry. In June 2021, a documentary play that I wrote together with Erika Hughes put Margot on the stage. For the title, *The Amazing Life of Margot Heuman*, I used a phrase that Margot repeated with a playful smile throughout our conversations: "I am amazing!" The play dramatizes in one act the conversations I had with Margot in April 2018. After I saw Margot one more time, she died on 11 May 2022 of old age. As a life-long reader of the *New York Times*, she would have appreciated being eulogized in an obituary that drew the attention of hundreds of thousands of readers.[32]

Queer Kinship

In queer studies, kinship is a central and established concept, reminding us to question biological reductivism.[33] "Families we choose," as the classic study by the anthropologist Kath Weston is aptly titled, shows how queer people reinvent and redefine family, an institution that can be violent and oppressive, particularly so to its queer members. Judith Butler has shown that kinship is a practice. Kinship, they argue, is vague and performative, rather than a biological "given."[34] Lauren Berlant has suggested understanding intimacy as a form of recognition of connection ("recognizing attachment"). Intimacy can encompass emotional ties but also physical ones; it can, but does not have to include desire and sexuality.[35] Stories of kinship and attachment beyond a canon, beyond a designated place, have a way of disappearing out of history.[36]

The shift from "family" to "kinship" is salient: kinship means networks of social relationships that have a narrow but important significance to society. Such relationships can stem from blood relations, marriage, or choice. Kinship means a family, but the term is more inclusive and not biologically predetermined. It can also mean people to whom we are connected by trust, intimacy, and affection.[37] This brief outline on queer kinship is possibly a banal fact to queer history readers, but probably new to those with a background in Holocaust and Jewish history where assumptions of biological family are still the norm.[38]

Holocaust history has much to gain in departing from omnipresent assumptions of "family" and taking "kinship" on board. Holocaust historians have addressed the fact that many Holocaust victims have created, and could survive thanks to, what Sibyl Milton has called "non-biological families."[39] Non-biological families, or rather kinship groups, emerged in two different ways: foremost, as biological families were ripped apart by deportation and extermination; however, many people moved to different units of their own accord as well, utilizing, or due to, the changes the Holocaust brought about. For instance, in Theresienstadt, many people sought the proximity of their friends who were in the same age group with whom they shared work, accommodation, or politics.[40] Children in the youth homes in this ghetto lived in kinship units, that is, room units with youth care workers, but also with friends. This separate kinship from their biological parents was an important factor that allowed the Theresienstadt children to experience the ghetto as a very different world from that of their parents. The notion of "non-biological families" in the Holocaust is problematic. Denoting kinship groups in the camps as "non-biological" inadvertently stresses an assumption that they were not "normal" and thus pathologizes them.[41] Queering kinship means reading the stories I present in this chapter outside of an established normative light. It means to look at the kinship units that emerged in the Holocaust decidedly not as a deviation from the norm (hence my critique of "non-biological families") but rather as a starting point for questioning the assumption that biological family is the norm.[42]

What did kinship mean in the victim society during the Holocaust? It existed in self-chosen or enforced groups of people who shared emotional support, confidential knowledge, and most importantly, resources. For some people this meant mutual intimacy; for others it meant confiding experiences of sexual violence or sexual barter. Kinship units could be long-lasting or short; the ties could come into being suddenly or be based on long-standing relationships through family, friendship, or a shared place of origin. Queering kinship in studying the Holocaust aids us in recognizing these relationships as a statement on what family and kinship are. We should thus take leave of the exceptionalist narrative of the Holocaust that sees these as anomalies.[43]

These theoretical insights on the conceptualization of kinship are extremely helpful in understanding Margot's kinship decisions. A particularly important moment was her choice to go with Dita at the July 1944 selection in Birkenau. Throughout her testimony, Margot repeated variations of the sentence, "Dita was my whole world."[44] We could read the moment in May 1944 when Margot wept on the train to Auschwitz, not because she finds herself in a cattle car on her way into the unknown but because of the pain of being separated from Dita, as the tipping point of her primary kinship's shift from her family to Dita. Margot's kinship definitively shifted in July 1944 when she decided to try to pass the selection to follow Dita; she did so because of Dita, not because of trying to survive. Here, her path separated from that of her family. The crying is salient as a marker of acknowledgment of loss or taking leave of kinship: be it Margot's crying on the train, or her father's crying when saying goodbye, or Margot's crying when she related the story to me in 2018. Finally, Margot's life also offers a complication to our perhaps ahistorical expectation of a "liberated" queer life. In the early 1950s, Margot chose to get married to a man and have a family. She felt she owed having children to her dead parents and sister. The bonds of her dead biological family had more weight for her than the queer life with Lu Burke and Greenwich Village. That did not mean that Margot's queerness stopped, or that she stopped acting on it. Margot made her life in layers of kinship units: that of her heterosexual husband and children, that of her queer lovers, and that of her work and colleagues.

Nate Leipciger

The history of Nate Leipciger, born in 1928 in Chorzów, Poland, complicates any notion that the history of same-sex relations in the concentration camps can be painted in an all too rosy light.[45] Leipciger grew up in a liberal orthodox household where his family went to the synagogue but did not keep kosher. He had one older sister. The family also had Polish non-Jewish friends. In September 1939, Chorzów again became Königshütte, annexed in the German regional district of Kattowitz, and soon after, the Leipcigers were forced to relocate to the nearby city of Sosnowiec where they were eventually forced into the Środula ghetto. Due to Nate's father's work for the Jewish police, the family was spared from transports for a relatively long time. Only in August 1943 were the Leipcigers deported to Auschwitz-Birkenau, where both his mother and sister were murdered. In October 1943, the Leipciger father and son were transferred to the newly constructed Groß-Rosen sub-camp Fünfteichen, just outside Breslau.[46] Here, Nate was designated to work inside the camp as an aid to an electrician and could thus avoid the gruelling work outside.

The room elder of the barrack in which Nate and his father were sleeping was a Polish gentile named Janek who made the then fifteen-year-old Leipciger his "pipel."[47] This word denoted child and teenage assistants to prisoner functionaries who were often sexually abused.[48] Janek was kind to Nate, gave him extra food, and put him up in a bed in his room. At first, Nate was pleased about the privileges – but soon, Janek used the proximity of Nate in his job for sexual assault. This was no accident: William Jones reminds us that most such relationships were initiated with sexual assault.[49] One night, Janek assaulted Nate, threatened him to make him stay silent, and ejaculated between Leipciger's thighs. Nate was ashamed and also afraid; he knew that sex

Figure 2.5. Photo of Nate Leipciger, September 1945.
Source: Courtesy of The Azrieli Foundation.

between men was punished by the camp SS. The second time, a few days later, Janek was with Nate alone when he came to the barrack before the men returned from work. He tried to force him to perform oral sex, and after Leipciger refused, Janek ordered Nate to pull down his trousers and raped him. "It was an embarrassing and painful experience," Leipciger recalled years later.[50]

In addition, the boy, whose knowledge of human reproduction was limited (Nate had read a few books on female physiology, but apparently his parents did not discuss conception with him), was worried that the rape could impregnate him. The following story took place between the first and the second assault: "The Polish prisoners suspected that Janek used me. They would tell stories that were meant for my ears. I pretended not to understand. They recounted an incident where a boy who was used as a woman conceived a child. I did not worry about it, as up to this point he [Janek] had not entered me. I also knew that to be impossible, but it still bothered me."[51] After the second assault, Leipciger's first reaction, as he described it, was related to his fear of pregnancy: "As soon as I got away from him, I rushed into the washroom to remove as much semen as possible. Even though I knew the stories of conception were false, at some level it had me frightened."[52] Of course, the impulse to wash off physical traces of his rapist is a universal response of rape victims, but it is worth noting how Leipciger recounted this traumatic assault. One can see just how young Leipciger was at the time by the photo taken of him after his liberation – the starvation makes him look young even for his age. As William Jones reminds us, Janek's approach to Nate was clearly a moment of grooming and child sex abuse.[53]

In the following weeks, Leipciger attempted to evade any interaction with Janek during the day, but there was nothing he could do about the attacks that came during the night. Leipciger never spoke of the assaults with his father, and he did not know if his father ever knew that they were occurring or not. What is startling, though, is that Leipciger recognized, and chose to tell, that the relationship with the functionary prisoner was "not without benefit."[54] He had access to better food as well as tobacco, which he used to barter for a new, appropriately fitting prisoner uniform, which in turn helped protect him from the violence of the other functionary prisoners.

In January 1944, Janek began a relationship with a new arrival, two years older than Nate, a boy of about seventeen. Leipciger's description of his reaction to this new relationship provides another surprising view of these moments of sexual violence: "I knew that my time as favorite was now totally up, which I somewhat regretted – it meant the kapo would not abuse me any longer, but it also meant that he withheld his affection. I was actually jealous of the other boy."[55] This quote includes several unexpected statements; alongside the sexual abuse, Leipciger unexpectedly and for the first time mentions the affection the kapo showed him. This affection must have been important for Leipciger, so important that he was jealous of his replacement.

Over time, the interactions between Janek and Nate developed from sexual assault to violent sexual barter.[56] Their connection began as an assault and rape, but with time became "one of the things one does to survive."[57] Historian Debórah Dwork suggests that the boy had a range of choices and so chose to use the relationship to secure his survival.[58] Jones places the relationship more within the scope of coercion than agency due to Leipciger's being a child.

I want to press on with some hard questions. Without discounting the important points about sexual abuse and grooming, I think that focusing on sexual violence sometimes shields us from discerning teenagers in the Holocaust as people with agency.[59] Focusing on the teenager's agency does not lessen the gravity of sexual violence that Janek inflicted on the boys he groomed and abused. Yes, Leipciger was a "poor kid making the best of a bad situation."[60] But in order to understand the victim experience in the concentration camps, we must understand that it was full of bad situations that most victims faced with poor odds. Focusing on agency allows us to understand how victims navigated these difficult and bad choices. The coerced relationship between

Janek and Leipciger is also a reminder to stop the use of "consent," because it is not an applicable category for most relationships in the Holocaust. Almost all relationships were marked by dependency, hierarchy, and violence, whether directly or indirectly. People's need to access protection and resources, and the omnipresent threat of violence and death, was too great to give them a free choice to walk away.[61]

Rather, we should probe the significance of Janek's affection to Leipciger and how Leipciger used the profits from the sexual barter to navigate the camp. The fact that in his later years Leipciger committed this story to paper and explicitly mentioned Janek's affection is meaningful.[62] Leipciger's father could not protect him, even though he was present. The father and son never spoke about the violent relationship. Thus, a form of kinship developed between the kapo and Leipciger – through a forbidden queer sexual practice that endangered both parties in the camps as well as through the provision of protection and sharing of resources. Leipciger's fear of becoming pregnant could also be interpreted as a form of recognition of this kinship. The biological unity between Leipciger and his father, meanwhile, faded into the background. Leipciger's frank discussion of the tangible advantages of sexual barter is to be understood as a meaningful moment of agency.

Leipciger had his first self-chosen and consensual sexual experiences only after the war. They were all heterosexual. Together with his father, he moved to Canada, where he married and had children. For years he asked himself whether the sexual abuse had influenced him or if it would turn him into a homosexual.[63] Like many abuse victims, he felt guilt and was ashamed of his experience. Inspired by the male survivors of Indian residential schools who courageously spoke out about sexual abuse, he was eventually able to share the experience of sexual abuse with his children and grandchildren. For Leipciger, writing about his experiences of sexual violence and sexual barter was "the most difficult narrative for [him] to tell."[64] Dorota Głowacka pointed out Nate's remarkable friendship with Theodor Fontaine, a former chief of the Sagkeeng Ojibwe First Nation in Manitoba and a survivor of Indian residential schools. Leipciger recognized a "commonality of suffering" that he shared with Fontaine, and after the publication of *The Weight of Freedom*, the two men spoke publicly together about their experiences of trauma and sexual abuse.[65] All these things – sharing the memories of trauma and sexual abuse with beloved family members, a validating friendship with a fellow survivor of sexual violence, and bearing testimony – allowed Leipciger a measure of closure and put an end to an extremely toxic kinship with his abuser.

Anne Frank

Anne Frank is probably the most famous victim of the Holocaust. Her diary comprises the life of a thoughtful, smart teenage girl during two years in hiding in Amsterdam. It is standard educational reading for many adolescents in the West – as well as a global source of inspiration for the oppressed.[66] Many details of Anne Frank's life are shown great attention: for example, the chestnut tree that she observed out the window while in hiding or the exact date of her death.[67] In January 2022 *The Betrayal of Anne Frank*, a collective new study about who betrayed people in

Figure 2.6. Photo of Anne Frank from 1942.
Source: Courtesy of the Anne Frank House.

the Hidden Annex, came out.[68] The book presented poorly researched speculation to rapt attention and large sales. It was also met with deep frustration by historians.[69]

It is therefore puzzling that one aspect, namely Anne Frank's queerness, has been to a great extent disregarded in academic literature and popular attention alike. Still, scholars such as the Canadian Cheryl Hann have presented key work.[70] While referencing Anne's queerness may be surprising to readers, they will likely be familiar with her relationship with Peter van Pels, who was three years older than Anne and one of the eight others in hiding with her. With remarkable regularity, queer journalists rediscover the diary entry from 6 January 1944;[71] however, there is hardly any analytical engagement with the passage.

I want to cite here the relevant passage from 6 January 1944 in full:

> I already had these kinds of feelings subconsciously before I came here, because I remember one night when I slept with Jacque [Jacqueline van Maarsen] I could not contain myself, I was so curious to see her body, which she always

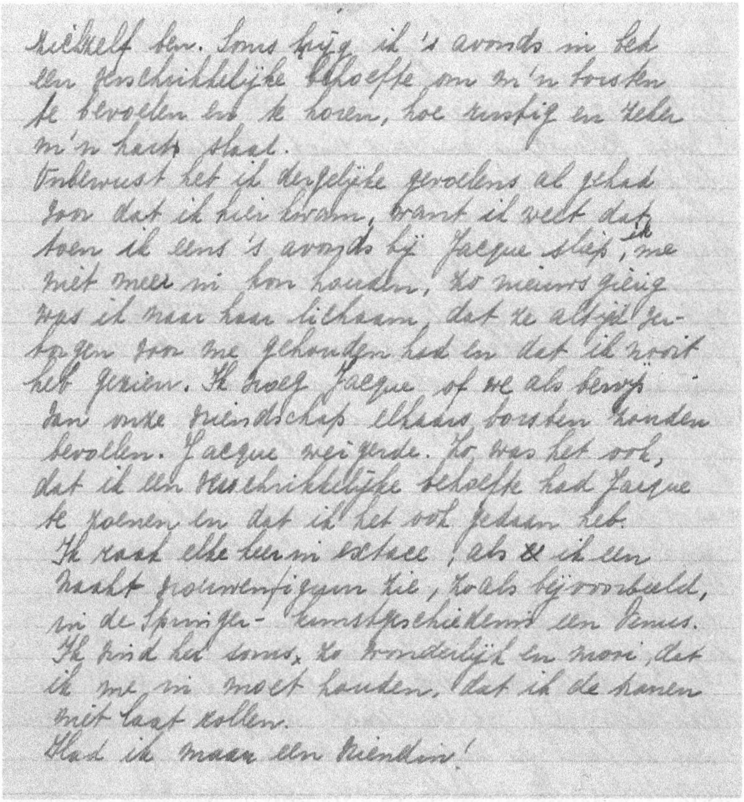
zelf ben. Soms krijg ik 's avonds in bed een verschrikkelijke behoefte om m'n borsten te bevoelen en te horen, hoe rustig en zeker m'n hart slaat.
Onbewust heb ik dergelijke gevoelens al gehad voor dat ik hier kwam, want ik weet dat toen ik eens 's avonds bij Jacque sliep, ik me niet meer in kon houden, zo nieuwsgierig was ik naar haar lichaam, dat ze altijd verborgen voor me gehouden had en dat ik nooit heb gezien. Ik vroeg Jacque of we als bewijs van onze vriendschap elkaars borsten konden bevoelen. Jacque weigerde. Zo was het ook, dat ik een verschrikkelijke behoefte had Jacque te zoenen en dat ik het ook gedaan heb.
Ik raak elke keer in extase, als ik een naakt vrouwenfiguur zie, zoals bijvoorbeeld, in de Springer-kunstgeschiedenis een Venus. Ik vind het soms, zo wonderlijk en mooi, dat ik me in moet houden, dat ik de tranen niet laat rollen.
Had ik maar een vriendin!

Figure 2.7. Page from Anne Frank's diary for 6 January 1944 in which she discusses her same-sex desire.

kept hidden from me and which I had never seen. I asked Jacque whether as a proof of our friendship we might feel one another's breasts. Jacque refused. I also had a terrible desire to kiss Jacque and that I did. I go into ecstasies every time I see the naked figure of a woman, such as Venus in the Springer History of Art, for example. It strikes me sometimes as so wonderful and exquisite that I have difficulty not letting the tears roll down my cheeks.

If only I had a girlfriend![72]

For context, in the same entry from 6 January 1944, Anne expresses her wish to speak about three sensitive topics: criticisms of her mother, same-sex desire, and her affection for Peter. As Cheryl Hann shows, the structure of the entry tempts one to neglect the queer moment: "Because Anne's exploration of her own queer desire is nested among supposed guarantors of heterosexuality, its weight – that is to say, its 'danger' – is obscured."[73] Nevertheless, neither Anne's wish to become a mother nor her relationship with Peter are grounds to neglect her queerness.

Hann's important work illuminates several instances in Anne Frank's diary that can be read as queer. In fact, one of the passages the cultural critic Allen Ellenzweig interprets as evidence that Anne was supposedly only "boy-crazy"[74] in the time before going into hiding itself contains a reference to the fact that although she enjoyed the attention of boys, she wanted nothing more than just that, their attention. When boys sought physical contact, Anne writes "they are definitely knocking on the wrong door."[75] Furthermore, Hann introduces a queer perspective on the mutual courting between Anne and Peter: the two wear the opposite sex's clothing. When Anne begins expressing her affection for Peter, she prefaces this affection with a reference to her relationship with Jacqueline, and before Anne mentions spending a dreamy, beautiful Saturday with Peter in the attic in March 1944, she recalls how Jacqueline taught her about sex.[76] Formulating this in the context of queer kinship, while Anne debates a new kinship with Peter, she contextualizes it with her old queer kinship with Jacqueline.

Queer desire was incidentally a topic that the Frank family did discuss, as Anne's biographer Melissa Müller pointed out already in 2013.[77] Anne had two gay uncles. Walter Holländer, her mother's brother who escaped to the US and survived, lived a closeted life.[78] There was, moreover, the flamboyant cousin of her father's, the French furniture designer Jean Michel Frank, who lived an openly gay life. He suffered from depression and died by suicide in American exile in 1941. About her uncle Walter, Anne remarked in a less than kind note on two pages that she later glued over – a place where she tried out gossip, lewd jokes, knowledge about sex work, and mixed in this remark: "All men, if they are normal, go with women, women like that accost them on the street and then they go together," she wrote. "In Paris they have big houses for that. Papa has been there. Uncle Walter is not normal."[79] The passage remained literally covered until scientists managed with the help of photoimaging software to read the page. In a way, the covering of these two pages is a fitting metaphor for the long-lasting invisibility of the queer themes of her diary.

All of this should not lead to the claim that Anne Frank was actually lesbian or bisexual.[80] Rather, my goal here is to show that Anne Frank, the iconic voice of Holocaust victims, expresses queer themes in not so thinly veiled terms in some of her diary passages. Whether she, if she had survived, would have lived as a heterosexual is not the point. Instead, Anne Frank reminds us of the need to take leave of the normative, binary division of heterosexuality and homosexuality (or alternatively bisexuality). This short discussion of queer themes in Anne Frank's diary illustrates the importance of queerness not so much as an identifying attribute as it is an analytical method.

Why are the queer aspects of Anne Frank's diary so little known? Cheryl Hann suggests that Anne's prominence is built upon her status as an innocent victim. Any sexualization – particularly queer sexualization as it is considered to be especially sexualized – would threaten this status. As the symbol of the innocence of all Holocaust victims, Anne must be distanced from her sexual autonomy, otherwise her innocence would be contaminated.[81] But beyond this, the post-war reception of Anne Frank's queerness was also characterized by unease. The eminent expert on Anne Frank, David Barnouw, notes how the first Dutch publisher of the diary, Gilles Pieter de Neve, removed mentions of Anne's menstruation as well as the passage from 6 January 1944.[82] This is odd, because Contact was a new, forward-thinking publisher that had published Fritz Kahn's progressive sex guide *Unser Geschlechtsleben* (Our sex life) before the Second World War. Otto Frank, Anne's father, did not approve of these changes, as he expressed in a letter to the English publisher's translator: "These were passages which were not printed in the Dutch edition because they were either too long or were likely to offend Dutch Puritan or Catholic susceptibilities."[83] Therefore, the passage from 6 January finally appeared in an only slightly abridged version in American and British publications of the English edition in 1952.

In 2017, the Anne Frank Fonds, the organization that Otto Frank founded and that is his universal heir, published a graphic novel adaptation of the diary. Edited by the director Ari Folman and illustrated by David Polonsky,

Figure 2.8. Page from the graphic novel adaptation of *The Diary of Anne Frank* by Ari Folman and David Polonsky.
Source: Courtesy of the Anne Frank Fonds.

the book presents the diary abbreviated on 149 illustrated pages. All of the text is based on actual entries. The adaptation includes the queer theme of 6 January 1944, on two pages, that is, three small panels on the bottom of one page and the whole page that follows.[84] In the panels, the illustrations depict the conversation that Anne recalled she had with Jacqueline. The images show two girls, one of whom has reached puberty, while the other has not: Jacqueline, resolutely rejecting Anne's suggestion to "show each other [their] breasts," clutches a teddy bear. In the following panel filling the opposite page, Anne walks through an alley of wisteria and ancient female naked statues towards a female figure waiting for her. The text says, "I must admit, every time I see a female nude, I go into ecstasy" and "If only I had a girlfriend!" Perhaps the most striking aspect of the illustration is that the statues seem to be alive. The goddesses stand guard, confidently showing off their grown-up curves, and smile at young Anne who walks through towards her girlfriend. The very same figure of Anne, walking towards a dream future, one she was not allowed to have, then closes the book.

Karl Marx's famous remark that history repeats itself, the first time as tragedy and second time as farce, applies here as well. The book bans in libraries that started spreading in the US in 2021, carried out by a group named Moms for Liberty, have been singling out queer literature as dangerous for children.[85] The book bans hit a nerve when a Tennessee library prohibited Art Spiegelman's *Maus* – the first visibly Jewish book to be singled out.[86] At first, Anne Frank's diary did not come under fire in its original version, but only in Folman and Polonsky's graphic adaptation. In October 2023, the book has been banned in three locations in Florida. Three places in Texas have either banned it briefly, fired a teacher who taught the book, or, in one district, restricted it to only older grade levels.[87] In Clay County, south of Jacksonville, Florida, a Jewish father succeeded in having all copies of Folman's adaptation removed from all grade level libraries.

The bottom-up dynamic of these book bans changed in March 2023, when the Florida Senate and House of Representatives passed the law HB 1069. This law restricts what children can learn about sexuality and gender in school.[88] Moreover, the bill permits parents to control their children's access to library books. In this vein, in January 2024, it was the original diary that was banned in Escambia County, Florida.[89] At that stage, publishers and PEN America moved to its defence. In August 2024, several large publishers led by Penguin Random House sued the state of Florida.[90]

How did we get to the strange place where the diary of Anne Frank, long seen as the a priori Holocaust literature for children, is considered not appropriate? It is thanks to its queer passages. The populist right-wing opponents challenging the book did not remember nor check that these passages were very much part and parcel of the original diary. Andrew Lapin, the journalist whose reporting has astutely followed the Anne Frank bans, observed: "They immediately suspected that it was the work of leftist indoctrination. They even suggested that the image of Anne Frank walking through the statue garden was pornographic." In fact, the queer passages in Anne Frank's diary, and the book per se, have become a symbol of the library bans for both the right and the left: "The responses you get are a lot of people on the left saying this is further proof that the entire book banning movement is absurd because they're banning Anne Frank. And then the people on the right are saying, this is just proof that nobody understands what we're all about because this isn't 'really Anne Frank.' This is a new 'perverted' version of Anne Frank."[91] One of the instances of the book bans specified that the queer passages of Anne Frank's diary "did not contribute to the themes of Holocaust education," and therefore the adaptation could be removed.[92]

Jacqueline van Maarsen, the girl with whom Anne was so enamoured, survived the war due to her parents' mixed marriage. She lived in Amsterdam until her death on 13 February 2025. She became known through her murdered friend and wrote five books about their friendship and her own experiences. David Barnouw shared with me that Jacqueline herself reportedly only read the 6 January 1944 passage in the 1990s and was "shocked."[93] Only in Van Maarsen's third book published in 2003, *My Name Is Anne, She Said, Anne Frank*, did she address her friend's affection. In a passage dedicated to this topic, which runs at more than a page, Van Maarsen went to great pains to avoid any description of the relationship as romantic or queer.[94] Van Maarsen stated that Anne was "effusive" and that she disregarded Jacqueline's boundaries. The attempt to touch each other's breasts, which "embarrassed [her] quite a bit," was for Van Maarsen "proof of [their] friendship," as opposed to an expression of sexual desire.[95] Embarrassment is the tone of the entire passage, in particular since Van Maarsen attempts to explain the intimate overture by Anne Frank's presumed interest in her bra as a piece of clothing that Anne, still flat-chested, did not wear yet. However, in an interview in 2004, Van Maarsen acknowledged that she and Anne shared "little secrets," including "sexual things."[96] Van Maarsen's version of the story as Anne being physically immature is both embarrassed and unkind. This renewed silencing of Anne Frank's queerness through the very person to whom she expressed such desire is a particular form of epistemological injustice.[97] It was probably not easy for someone of Van Maarsen's generation and habitus of "compulsory heterosexuality" to address the queer desire that she was the object of.[98] Jacqueline van Maarsen became noteworthy due to her dead friend; we should make space for the queer desire that her friend felt for her.

Anne Frank's queerness is salient for our understanding of the "real" Anne Frank. For a contemporary young audience, queer protagonists are crucial but also matter of fact. Queerness makes Anne more relatable; it humanizes her. Andrew Lapin pointed out that it is, moreover, the queer aspect that gives people like the literature freedom activists a new reason to stand guard for Anne Frank, to advocate for her because they recognize that she is being caught up in this due to the broader fear of and attack on books with queer identities.[99] In this respect, Anne Frank's diary is a strong example of queer kinship between the past and today.

Molly Applebaum

Molly Applebaum's unique diary offers a rare glimpse into a possible lived reality of the anecdote by Joan Nestle that opens this chapter.[100] Born in October 1930 in Krakow as Melania Weissenberg, Molly grew up in an assimilated Jewish family.[101] Her father died and her mother remarried. In

Figure 2.9. Photo of Melania Weissenberg from 1942, titled "Molly Applebaum, 1939" in the collection of the Azrieli Foundation.

Source: Courtesy of The Azrieli Foundation.

1940, her family moved to the small town of Dąbrowa Tarnowska, eighty kilometres from Krakow, where they hoped to be supported by her aunt and where, in contrast to Krakow, there was an open ghetto.[102] In March 1942, at eleven years and six months of age, Melania began to write her diary. This self-testimony is well known to Holocaust scholars, particularly because of the ambivalent sexual relationship she had with an older Polish farmer who hid her.[103] This heterosexual connection, however, should not cloud our view of Melania's earlier love for a woman.

In her diary, Applebaum wrote about life in the ghetto and her twenty-year-old friend Sabina Goldman. Sabina was an employee of the Jewish Social Self-Help. Melania fell in love with Sabina, and her diary is full of comments that express this love, such as that from April 1942:

> If only you knew, Bineczka, how much I love you ... Oh, if only you knew. But you do not and you shall never know.

> Because you will not believe that such a love can exist. It is called lesbian love; that is, of a woman for another woman. I love you with all my naive, still entirely pure, tiny heart. And I am suffering. And you are my first love. What a pity that I cannot give you telling proofs of my love! Consequently, the ones I can give must suffice. If only I could do something for you ... But you do not ask anything of me, because you do not think me capable of anything. But do know this, my beloved Bineńka, my love for you can accomplish much. Remember that you can always count on me, no matter what.[104]

This diary entry provides several important perspectives on the queerness of Jewish adolescents during the Holocaust; Molly speaks clearly about her love for Sabina and labels it also as "lesbian love." It is notable that the eleven-year-old Molly knew of this terminology. At the same time, she also recognized that Sabina had no understanding of such lesbian love because she did not think in these categories and it was therefore impossible for Sabina to acknowledge Molly's affection as romantic. Perhaps the fact that Molly came from the big city of Krakow while Sabina grew up in a small town had something to do with it. Had Molly, like Joan Nestle's acquaintance, heard of or read *The Well of Loneliness*? We can only speculate. In addition, Molly was well aware of the age difference between the two and she could not see herself as an equal partner to her friend; considering the love of an eleven-year-old for a twenty-year-old, this is not particularly astounding. It is, however, notable that Molly in no way saw herself as powerless and throughout this experience acted with agency. This observation corresponds with the findings of historians of childhood.[105]

Sabina and Molly were separated in September 1942 when Molly and her cousin escaped into hiding. Sabina wrote to Molly when she was already in hiding, saying that she could not leave her parents.[106] But a few days later, Sabina did separate from her parents and tried to run for her life. As German police forces liquidated the ghetto and deported its inhabitants, Sabina attempted to flee but was arrested by Polish police and deported to the Belzec extermination camp where she was murdered.[107] Molly survived in hiding with her cousin between September 1942 and January 1944. For a long time, she wrote in her diary of how much she missed Sabina, "the creature I love the most in the world," mentioning her here in 1942 and again in February 1943.[108] Some of the few things she could preserve while in hiding were letters and photos of Sabina. (These were apparently more important than photos of herself, at least. No photos of Applebaum from this time have survived.) In one of these photos, Sabina Goldman and her sister Mancia can be seen; on the reverse an inscription states, "For dearest Melina, as a reminder of Mancia." Sabina's inscription reads, "to the beloved Mela, Sabina G."[109]

After the war, Molly planned to build a memorial room for Sabina and even completed a preliminary sketch for it.[110] She also met Sabina's father, who survived. He lamented that he did not have any photos of his murdered family, yet Molly did not reveal that she had such photos in her possession. Decades later, in the testimony she wrote for her children, she explained how important these photos were to her both in the past and the present: "And there I was, listening and taking this all in, but I did not divulge the fact

Figure 2.10. Photo of Sabina Goldman (right) and her sister Mania (left). 2016.442.1, Melania Weissenberg papers, United States Holocaust Memorial Museum Archives, Washington, DC.

that I was in possession of a few snapshots of Sabina and her sister. I can only think, now, that I was afraid I would be asked to give them up, and I was not prepared to take that chance. I have these photos to this day."[111]

Here, we can again recognize a queer kinship in the multiple instances in which Melania designated Sabina as her favourite person in the world, mourned their separation, and lamented her death. This is even clearer in the moment in which Molly held on to the only surviving photographs of her murdered friend instead of sharing them with Sabina's father. In keeping these photos secret, she held and thus kept a unique ownership of Sabina, placing herself above her father, the only surviving member of her friend's family.

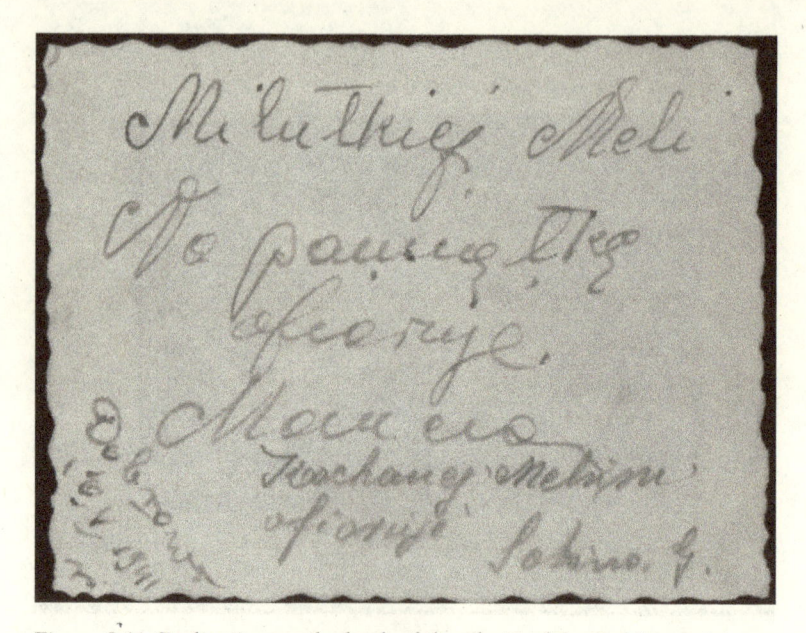

Figure 2.11. Dedication on the back of the photo of the Goldman sisters. 2016.442.1, Melania Weissenberg papers, United States Holocaust Memorial Museum Archives, Washington, DC.

Proprietorial as this claim was, its possessiveness is also a feature of kinship. Molly's decisions to designate Sabina as the most important person in her life, to mourn her loss, and to remain the keeper of the only pictorial documents of her memory are all important expressions of Molly's agency in enacting queer kinship.

Molly emigrated to Canada in 1948 and married a fellow Polish survivor two years later. In her memoir, she explains that she liked her future husband, but did not love him; she was attracted to his aunt and her family, who were affectionate and warm, while she was alone.[112]

They had three children, two girls and a boy. Unfortunately, the marriage was difficult; Molly's husband was

Figure 2.12. Photo of Molly Applebaum with two children in the 1950s.
Source: Courtesy of Sharon Wrock.

"verbally abusive."[113] In her memoir, Molly spends several pages discussing how abusive, stingy, angry, and hostile her husband was.[114] When he died in 1983, Molly got some closure by selling the house and moving elsewhere, and later by reading literature about abusive relationships. In her memoir, there is a palpable sense of melancholy that Molly did not choose to leave, or push back, that she let the relationship diminish her for decades, so much so that it is nearly the note on which she ends.

What remains of Molly's love for Sabina? Sabina's inscription on the back of the photo is viewable on the website of the United States Holocaust Memorial Museum. Sabina is, however, mistakenly reported as Melania's cousin, and with this description Melania's queer love is cut out of the narrative – a situation that remains unchanged two years after I contacted the archive. Melania's diary was published in 2018 in a loving edition by the Canadian Azrieli

Foundation. The detailed introduction from Jan Grabowski only hints at the queer themes contained in the diary but does not address them.[115] The Holocaust literature scholar Sara Horowitz addresses Molly's infatuation with Sabina, but she contextualizes it as "polysemous eroticism of adolescence" without investigating queer themes further.[116]

Molly Applebaum's story in many ways contributes to themes of queer kinship, agency, ability to find a language to name one's desire, and post-war compromises. Reading Molly's memoir, it is striking that unlike in her diary, she never calls her feelings for Sabina "love," but gives her so much attention, and speaks of her so affectionately, that she makes that point nevertheless. It is improbable that Molly is aware of the concept of queer kinship, but nevertheless she organizes her bond with Sabina in that way: whether it is when she discusses Sabina's letters and photos that she kept, or when she comments on Sabina's decision whether to die with her parents or try to survive. There is something profoundly melancholy about the fact that Molly describes herself as agentic during the Holocaust, whether in relationship with Sabina or in hiding, but as powerless and passive in her abusive post-war marriage. However, Molly was able to reclaim her agency: she wrote her memoir, spoke her truth, and now has the captive attention of Holocaust and queer historians alike.

Jiří Vrba

The history of Jiří Vrba is, in the context of this chapter, noteworthy in three ways: his is the only Czech testimony despite being imprisoned at the same time as Margot

Heuman in both Theresienstadt and the Family Camp in Auschwitz; born in 1924, he was slightly older than the other survivors described here; and finally, he has lived his entire life as a self-identifying gay man – perhaps not in the way we would imagine a "queer life" today, but in the context of the time, Vrba's refusal to live in the closet was remarkable.

Despite the fact that we know much about Vrba's life – there is a literary estate containing memories of his friends and companions – there is no testimony from Vrba at my disposal in which he speaks of his own sexuality.[117] Consequently, Vrba stands in contrast to the other four protagonists of this chapter, all of whom left behind their own testimony in which they dealt with their own queer experiences. I see this gap in the sources as a challenge to show what we can know and what we can speculate about as a methodological exercise in queer history.

Jiří Vrba was many things at sixty-nine years of age: a Jew and Holocaust survivor, a gay man, a Communist, a creative artist, and an organizer of cultural events and exchanges. He was also an informer of the secret state police in Communist Czechoslovakia (StB). I do not want readers to use this information to delegitimize Jewish or queer history; but that is no reason not to tell his story nor to suppress the fact that he was an informant of the secret police. I tell the whole story, showing how Vrba's collaboration with the StB is but one of many facets of this fascinating man.

I came across Vrba in 2010 while researching for my dissertation. Struck by the silences in the Visual History Archive, I began to consider the notable lack of Holocaust testimonies that included transgressive sexualities. I asked

Figure 2.13. Photo of Jiří Vrba from the 1990s. Courtesy of the Jewish Museum in Prague.

the then archivist of the oral history collection at the Jewish Museum in Prague, Hermína Neuner, to send me any testimonies in the collection that made any mention of "homosexuality." These testimonies remained carefully stored on my external hard drive until 2018, by which time I had long been working on the topic of queer Holocaust history. One day I remembered this hard drive, finally went through the texts, and lo and behold, found in the testimony of a man from Brno the following statement about his time in Terezín: "I learned a lot, I was reading lots, I had excellent friends, one of them was Jiří Vrba, today he's dead. Apart from the fact that he was a homosexual, he was also a person who read widely, he was very knowledgeable, and I learned from him much."[118]

I searched for information on Vrba and discovered that he was one of the founders of the Terezín Initiative, the association of Czech Holocaust survivors. He was also the guiding spirit behind the celebration of cultural life in Theresienstadt from 1989 on. In 2014, the then director of the Jewish Museum in Prague, Leo Pavlát, delivered a poignant remembrance of Vrba on the radio.[119] Jana Šplíchalová, another friend from the Jewish Museum, informed me in 2018 that the institution held an entire collection on Vrba. I wondered to myself how it was that I, who at that point had finished writing a book manuscript on Theresienstadt, was hearing for the first time of the man who was obviously *the* mover and shaker of all things Theresienstadt in his time?[120] The answer, I believe, lies in the intersectional nature of his identity: he was Jewish, gay, and he worked for the StB. After Vrba died in 1993, he was almost completely forgotten because in the Czech context, he belonged to several undesired histories.

The Vrbas were a comfortably middle-class Prague family. Jiří's father, Adolf, was from Kutná Hora and worked as a goldsmith, representing a Swiss watch firm.[121] He is said to have liked to overstate his own importance. Jiří's mother, Marta, née Hermannová, was from Prague and was a typical "Jewish mother."[122] Born in 1924, Jiří was the youngest child, with two older siblings, a brother, Karel, born in 1918 and a sister, Eva, born in 1921. The Vrbas were a Czech-speaking family. Jiří and his siblings spent their childhood in the Žižkov district of Prague before the family moved to Vodičkova Street in the city centre. Jiří attended the English Real Gymnasium before he was forced to leave school in 1939 because he was a Jew, after which he began an apprenticeship learning goldsmithing. In the same year, Eva escaped to England on a Kindertransport.[123]

In December 1941, the family was put on one of the first transports to Theresienstadt. Here, Adolf became the barrack elder of the Hohenelbe barracks, the Hospital, and later, the Kavalier barracks next door where the mentally ill were housed.[124] Karel worked as a nurse; what Marta did in the ghetto we do not know. Jiří was seventeen at the time and was therefore placed in one of the children's homes, where he would remain for the entirety of his two and a half years in Theresienstadt. Fredy Hirsch, the beloved, gay deputy director of the Youth Care Department, also lived in this home on the ground floor.[125] Vrba worked as a goldsmith in the Jeweller's Workshop, one of the SS's forced labour detachments in which workers made pendants from silver according to a model.[126] In 1942, everyone in this workshop was arrested because the SS suspected the workers of stealing some of the silver they were working with; in reality, it was one of the German guards who was actually guilty.[127] Later, Vrba was assigned to the labour detachment responsible for building the South barracks on the Bohušovice meadow.

Vrba's only romantic relationship in Theresienstadt was with a girl two years younger than he, Eva Komínıková, who was also from Prague. Eva worked in Lautschárna, a workshop next to the Jeweller's Workshop; there, she came to know Jiří. Eva liked the attractive, curly haired eighteen-year-old Jiří, but what most impressed her was how educated and well-read he was. The two officially became a couple at a small party hosted in Jiří's room

Figure 2.14. Photo of Jiří Vrba from 1946.
Source: Courtesy of the author.

attended by Eva and another girl on New Year's Eve 1942/3. Jiří would track down much coveted theatre tickets and take Eva to see several of the ghetto performances that are now famous: *The Bartered Bride*, Verdi's *Requiem*, and Karel Švenk's *Dasselbe in Grün*. Thereafter, Vrba began organizing performances of his own. In early 1942, he prepared a reimagination of Esther for the children in the hospital, which he and Páťa Fischel directed together.[128] In June 1942, when a rumour swept through the ghetto that the Nazis had murdered the famous Czech poet and writer Vítězslav Nezval, Vrba put together an evening dedicated to Nezval's work.[129] Vrba had his first sexual experience at eighteen with Eva.[130]

Vrba was also a member of the secret Communist Party in Theresienstadt.[131] In the 1930s, he had been deeply influenced by his uncle Richard Kraus, an engineer active as a singer in Berlin who later left to fight in the Spanish International Brigades.[132] In 1941, Kraus was arrested for distribution of Communist leaflets. The Nazis imprisoned him in Dachau and Buchenwald, before murdering him during the 14f13 Action in 1942.[133] Vrba's friendship with another Communist, his cousin Otto Šling, would be quite consequential for him after the war. Vrba reflected on the strict secrecy of the party's work and how it operated in cells of always only three members. The other members of his cell were Jiří Kosta and Zdeněk Kárný, the younger brother of the Czech historian and writer Miroslav Kárný. Zdeněk was later killed in Auschwitz.[134] In 1988, Vrba recalled his illegal Communist activity: "There was a pronounced illegal political life. ... In 1942, I joined the Czechoslovak Communist Party in Terezín. I remember, how quickly we reacted when a rumour was making rounds that [the poet Vítězslav] Nezval was executed. We decided to make a cultural event from his work. We included monologues as well as dialogues accompanied by songs."[135]

In May 1944, the Vrbas were deported on the last of the three May transports to the Theresienstadt Family Camp in Birkenau. The child care in this camp, two individual barracks of the Family Camp established by Fredy Hirsch, is well known, and Vrba would become one of the caregivers in these barracks – all the while never knowing that one of his colleagues was Margot Heuman. His first encounter with children in Auschwitz, who in Theresienstadt were relatively well looked after, rattled Vrba. He recalls, "The encounter with them was cruel, they looked to us terrible, and we realized what was expecting us."[136]

At the beginning of July 1944, the SS liquidated the Family Camp, and all of the Vrbas managed to survive the selection.[137] His mother was sent to the women's camp in Birkenau and from there on to Stutthof. After spending several days in the men's camp in Birkenau, Jiří, his brother, and his father were all transferred to Blechhammer for forced labour.[138] Blechhammer was the second-largest sub-camp of Auschwitz; prisoners were forced to march five kilometres twice a day from the camp to the factory where they manufactured synthetic gasoline.

It was either in the men's camp in Auschwitz or in Blechhammer that Vrba had his first queer experience. In 2018, Vrba's partner Miroslav Spořitel explained to me how a twenty-year-old Jiří came to know and love a French prisoner whom he shared a bunk with. The two were so exhausted that they only ever cuddled and caressed one other – for anything more they were both too weak. At some point, the pair was separated when Vrba moved camps. Even though his lover knew no other language than French, and Vrba in turn could not speak it, the Frenchman still managed to tell Vrba that should he survive, he should look for him on the avenue de Wagram in Paris.[139] Significantly, Vrba never bore testimony about this moment in any official capacity; he only confided it to his partner. Was it that he did not feel his first queer experience was the "right" matter for the archives? Perhaps he internalized the rules of the "epistemology of the closet," in which queer experiences did not warrant being a part of recorded history.

Vrba was lucky, and survived. In January 1945, the Germans sent almost all surviving inmates of Blechhammer on death marches to Buchenwald. Jiří and his brother Karel survived, although their father was among those prisoners to die a few days after arrival.[140] In Buchenwald, Jiří was lucky to become the block writer in the Children's Block 66, overseen by the well-known Czech Communist Antonín Kalina.[141] After liberation, Vrba's first stop was Paris.[142] He discovered that the avenue de Wagram is one of the eleven majestic boulevards built by the architect Georges-Eugène Haussmann that converge on the Arc de Triomphe. I visited the avenue de Wagram in April 2019 while a visiting professor in Paris. The street runs five hundred metres to the north-east, and the houses that line it are all five stories or taller. In the early summer of 1945, the survivor Jiří Vrba strolled along the very same street in search of his lover. He did not find him. He did, however, return to Czechoslovakia as a self-identifying gay man.

His new start in Czechoslovakia was difficult. His mother was one of the many Stutthof prisoners who were murdered by the Germans in February 1945 as they cleared out the camp on the shores of the Baltic Sea.[143] Strangers now lived in their old apartment on Vodičkova Street, and the neighbours his parents had given their family heirlooms to for protection did not want to give them back.[144] In August 1945, his sister Eva returned from England. In an oral testimony given to the VHA, she recalled how when she asked one of her brothers what she should bring with her from England for him, he answered that he needed everything but a toothbrush.[145] Perhaps for these reasons, Jiří settled in Brno and not in his native Prague.

Jiří made his career in the Communist Youth Union in Brno and later worked in the union's Central Committee in Prague. In 1952, during the antisemitic Slánský trials, he was dismissed.[146] Whether this was due to his Jewishness, or whether his relation to his cousin and politician Otto Šling played a role, we do not know for certain. Vrba believed that the decisive factor was his connection to Šling, who was also a friend. From 1953, Vrba worked for three years as a labourer in a factory, and in 1956 he managed to secure a foothold in theatre in Karlovy Vary. Later, he was instrumental in the creation of the famous Semafor Theatre in Prague, and he led the theatre as its director until 1963.[147] He often brought his niece Zuzana, his brother's daughter, a singer who recorded several songs including the classic "Sluníčko," there.[148]

Vrba had several partners. Zuzana remembers that Jiří often stayed overnight at her parents' house in Prague, occasionally bringing a friend with him. In 1966, Vrba worked in theatre directing in Ostrava where he met the seventeen-years-younger actor Miroslav Spořitel. Miroslav had divorced after a short marriage and had a son, although he knew even before his marriage that he was gay. Vrba and Spořitel's relationship would continue until Vrba's death. Zuzana recalls how Vrba had once defended Spořitel to her: "Miroslav came to visit every day, and I did not like it. I did not understand why he sits there every day, since Jirka lived with us at that time, and I was being obnoxious ... I would say things like, 'Why is he here again?' and my uncle took me to the side and very clearly told me, as long as I am staying with you, Miroslav will be here as well."[149]

Zuzana and her cousin explained to me that Jiří's homosexuality was never discussed in the family. It took some time before they realized that their uncle was gay. Vrba brought Spořitel to meet the family, introducing him first to his brother, with whom he had a close relationship. His sister was uncomfortable with Jiří's sexuality and for years did not allow him to visit.[150] Eventually, the sister decided to accept Vrba and only then the family welcomed Spořitel. Vrba was enormously grateful to his sister. Afterwards, Vrba and Spořitel were simply another couple that exchanged endearments like "my sweetheart" at family parties.[151] Vrba let his friends know that he was living with a man, and he was also open about the fact with the secret police.

Then, and this is the most difficult aspect of his biography, Vrba collaborated with the secret police.[152] Evidently, he was recruited in 1954 for an operation against homosexuals after he himself had been arrested for the same reason a year before.[153] Homosexuality was a prosecutable offense until 1961 in Czechoslovakia.[154] But for the entire duration of the socialist era in Czechoslovakia, queerness was a risk that made people liable to blackmail. This was also the reason why some gay men agreed to cooperate with the secret police.[155]

Vrba was not the only Czech Holocaust survivor who became, in some manner and for some time, an informer for the secret police. So was Miroslav Kárný, one of the leaders of the Communist Party in Theresienstadt and the later eminent historian of the Czech Holocaust.[156] Another survivor, the historian Toman Brod, also worked for six years with the secret police.[157] Both of them were "forgiven" – to date, they are appreciated and celebrated. What sets them apart from Vrba is their manifest heterosexuality: Vrba was forgotten due to his intersectionality of "offenses," not only informing but also queerness. Vrba worked as an informer with some interruptions for the entire existence of the Socialist regime, including after his dismissal from the Communist Party in 1969. He spied on his friends, such as the well-known former Communist and dissident Marie Švermová, as well as her daughter and son-in-law, Jiřina Kopoldová und Bedřich Kopold.[158] Vrba was also prepared to spy on leftist Czech intellectuals who had fled into exile in other countries.[159]

Why did Vrba work for the secret state police? We will never know exactly. I believe that Vrba was an informer because he remained an ardent Communist and was attached to power. Vrba let those around him believe that he was a critic of the Communist regime before and after 1989.[160] However, to the secret police and, more importantly, to his partner, he made it clear he was a Communist – and that remained true after 1989. This "higher moral ground" was, for him, the reason for his collaboration, even if that meant residence outside of the country away from his beloved partner.[161] Vrba had many opportunities to emigrate post-1968; he spent a year in the West German city of Trier, where he, incidentally, was nearly beaten to death by a neo-Nazi. At the thought of "staying in the West," however, he broke down.[162]

Vrba was also a man conscious of power. Another Czech Jewish survivor, Miloš Povondra, who arrived in Buchenwald in early 1945, remembered Vrba as a relentless block elder in one of the barracks for Jewish prisoners.[163]

Significantly, when Vrba spoke with an American writer in 1989 about his imprisonment in Buchenwald, he claimed that he worked in the quarry.[164] Vrba's career as a theatre director did not develop as he hoped – he worked on regional stages. He was also fired in the Olomouc theatre in 1978. The collaboration with the secret police gave him the opportunity to have influence.[165] But at the same time, a strong factor of working for the secret police was fear.[166] Vrba was keenly aware how lucky he was not to become a victim of the trial surrounding his cousin Šling. Even though he lived, for his time, a relatively out life (both his family and close friends and colleagues knew that he was gay), it is reasonable to assume that Vrba's run-in with the police in 1954 when homosexuality was still a criminal offense left long-lasting traces.

Shortly before the "Velvet Revolution," Vrba became interested in Terezín. He gave an interview to the oral history collection at the Theresienstadt Memorial and befriended Jiří Lauscher, who survived the ghetto himself and organized much of the commemorative activity.[167] After 1989, Vrba had a time of great prosperity and productivity. When one looks at all he succeeded in building from the ground up in only four years, one can hardly believe it. Vrba was one of the founders of the Terezín Initiative; he organized exchanges with Israel; he had a leading position in the Pragokoncert, a leading Czech music agency; and it is thanks to him that people began to celebrate the memory of Theresienstadt's thriving cultural life, above all the children's performance of *Brundibár*. He made a deep impression on the documentarian Martin Šmok, then a young

Figure 2.15. Photo of Jiří Vrba showing the Bratislava synagogue to Edward Serotta in 1989.
Source: Courtesy of Edward Serotta.

man, who recalls of Vrba, "He was definitively not afraid to discuss topics that others avoided – and yet others, who made out of their survival a sense of self-importance, stayed away from him. He was different, very much so, and I do not only mean him being gay."[168]

Vrba died on 25 December 1993. He had a heart attack and was taken to the hospital where Spořitel visited him. Vrba, who knew that he would not be coming back, tried to hold his partner's hand, but Spořitel was ashamed to be seen by the medical personnel and pushed Vrba's hand away. The next day, Vrba was dead; he was sixty-nine years old. Whether his early death was related to his experiences in the concentration camps; whether he, like his brother who suffered several infarctions and died at sixty-two, died of natural causes; or whether Vrba worked himself to death with the hectic tempo of the last four years of his life; or whether he was anxious about the appearance of the lists of the unofficial informers of the secret police that started coming out a year earlier – that we will also never know.

In the end, Vrba's legacy is one of a fascinating but ambivalent man who laid the groundwork for much of today's knowledge of Terezín, Czech Jewish history, and Czech culture. He lived, in the context of the time, a relatively open queer life. Those around him knew that he was gay and got to know his partner. Moreover, thanks to his persistence and willingness to make compromises, Vrba's relatives even accepted Spořitel as his husband and next of kin. Spořitel was listed as one of the bereaved in his obituary.[169] Vrba's willingness to accommodate his sister's homophobia, in his gratitude when she came around and was willing to include him with his partner (rather than a more understandable anger), shows that the choice of queer kinship was not an easy one for a Holocaust survivor who had but few biological family members. We may celebrate queer kinship as an emancipatory move, yet for many queer Holocaust survivors missing their dead biological relatives, it was not an emotionally meaningful choice. Similar to Margot Heuman, Vrba lived a self-chosen post-war life of compromise between queer and biological kinship. In all these respects, Vrba may not be the heroic figure of queer history that some wish queer people of the past to be. Yet when I reflect on his life, his accomplishments, and his retreat into oblivion, I see that he was in many ways a signpost for queer

Holocaust history, with his fractures, ambivalences, and contradictions.

Just before the "Velvet Revolution" in November 1989, Vrba befriended Edward Serotta, a Jewish American writer and photographer who travelled Eastern Europe to document Jewish life here. Serotta had been living in Budapest since March 1988, making him a bit of an outlier, since almost no other Westerners were living in Warsaw Pact countries then. Serotta hired Vrba to be his guide and interpreter. They spent several days in June 1989 travelling by car from the west to the east of Czechoslovakia, from Prague to Brno, Bratislava, Trnava, Nitra, and Košice. Vrba was charming, full of stories, and had excellent networks at his disposal; his English was excellent, more than making up for the fact that he had no sense of direction, a tangible drawback while driving around in an era before GPS.[170] Serotta went on to write about Vrba in his classic account, *Out of the Shadows*.[171] This encounter turned out to be a prescient anecdote of both this chapter and book: Serotta was aware that many of the Czech and Slovak Jews whom he met were informers for the secret police and in fact reported on him, and he touched on that topic in his book.[172] During his travels in the late 1980s, Serotta was aware that he was attracted to men, but he only embraced that desire as an identity years later. But his queerness was enough for him to recognize that Vrba was a gay man, without either of them discussing the topic openly. Serotta did not ask Vrba, and Vrba did not acknowledge either his homosexuality or his partner.[173] Serotta went on to set up and run Centropa, an archive and educational tool about twentieth-century Central and Eastern European Jewish memory. Among the over one thousand interviews Centropa collected between 2000 and 2009, not one person spoke about their own queerness.[174] I do not bring up this queer silencing as a reproach of Centropa or of Serotta, whose work I, and many Central European Jewish historians, benefit from. Rather, I present the encounter between these two Jewish gay men as closing evidence of the importance of matters that we do not see until we are told we should see and write about them.

Conclusion

There are three motives in these stories: the issues of sexual identity and its boundaries, obliterated history, and queer kinship. We do not do justice to any of these survivors by characterizing them through statements such as "she loved women" or "he was gay." According to Laura Doan, such a characterization of historical subjects would be dubious because they are completely the product of remembrance and not history.[175] To denote these people as lesbian or gay is an ahistorical interpretation rendered by our own contemporary perspective which bypasses historical reality. Instead, I attempt to show how we can observe the emergence of queer desire and a queer form of kinship during the Holocaust. Indeed, Margot Heuman understood herself as lesbian, and Jiří Vrba saw himself as a gay man. But we cannot say the same of Margot's great love Dita, nor of Anne Frank or Molly Applebaum.

Of course, Leipciger's experience of abuse did not render "him" anything in terms of sexual orientation. Instead of questioning ahistorical sexual identities, we should seek out queer practices. Nate Leipciger's history illustrates the dimensions of sexual violence and exploitation in some (and perhaps many) relationships during the Holocaust.[176] We most certainly cannot call him a homosexual. Leipciger reports that he learned to accept the enforced relationship. Nevertheless, the sexual violence he suffered cast long shadows in his life; for decades he was traumatized by the abuse, feeling ashamed and remaining silent.

Similar silence manifests itself in a different form in the silencing of queer desire. Margot Heuman, Anne Frank, and Molly Applebaum provided clear descriptions of their own queerness, descriptions which Holocaust studies has not wanted to take seriously. As Cheryl Hann argues, this is an epistemological injustice.[177] All three girls are considered to be important voices of the Holocaust; however, their queerness remains largely invisible. If the queer content of their self-testimonies were known, they would be excluded from the ranks of well-known voices.[178] By refusing to acknowledge the same-sex desire in these accounts, we may be silencing queer voices. In a different way, this erasure applied to Vrba, too: he was known as a gay man, and that circumstance was a decisive factor in the very forgetting of his person. By not being a part of accepted Holocaust history, these people lose their historical belonging and disappear.[179] People without history are dust.

Kinship through a queer lens enables us to read the decisions of and possibilities for choice available to Holocaust victims in a historical context, upending the heteronormative view of "real family" vs "non-biological family." The concept reveals agency, mentalities, and relationships that developed during the Holocaust, and within them there is room for ambivalence and difficult stories.[180] Historians have been discussing what we should do with problematic findings about queer protagonists, with the racism of Magnus Hirschfeld and Radclyffe Hall, or the Nazi background of a well-known Berlin bar owner.[181] We are well advised to strive towards an open, inclusive history that is not afraid of making space for uncomfortable findings.

Notes

1. Towards a Queer History of the Holocaust

1 Since the original publication, several authors have followed suit: Sienna, *A Rainbow Thread*; Glowacka, "Sexual Violence against Men and Boys"; Rautenberg, *Homophobia in the Nazi Camps*; Schüler-Springorum, "Homophobe Erinnerungen"; Zabransky, "Male Jewish Teenage Sexuality"; Nunn, "Trans Liminality"; Marhoefer, "Transgender Life."
2 Key studies include: Schoppmann, *Zeit der Maskierung*; Van Dijk, *Einsam war ich nie*; Grau, *Homosexualität in der NS-Zeit*; Giles, "Legislating Homophobia in the Third Reich"; Spurlin, *Lost Intimacies*; Evans, "Why Queer German History?"
3 Crenshaw, "Mapping the Margins"; see also Schraub, "White Jews."
4 This was despite the liberalization of laws concerning homosexuality in the interwar period in Central Europe. The research on interwar queer life and the push for decriminalization is rich; key studies include: Rieder, *Heimliches Begehren*; Seidl, Wintr, and Nozar, *Od žaláře k oltáři*; Lybeck, *Desiring Emancipation*; Beachy, *Gay Berlin*; Marhoefer, *Sex and the Weimar Republic*; Pająk, "Echo Texts"; Samper Vendrell, *The Seduction of Youth*; Kurimay, *Queer Budapest*; Marhoefer, *Racism and the Making of Gay Rights*.
5 Eschebach, "Geschichte und Gedenken," 65. See also Janz, "Zeugnisse überlebender Frauen"; and Gelbin, "Double Visions."
6 Cantillon, "Challenging the Shame Paradigm."
7 In his *Rain of Ash*, Ari Joskowicz posed a similar question in his examination of how the Porajmos was told, skewed, and silenced from the Jewish perspective.

8 Evans, "Why Queer German History?" 371; Rubin, "Epilogue: Doing Straight Time."
9 Hájková, "Sexual Barter in Times of Genocide"; Ley, "Sexualität im Männer-KZ."
10 For these, see Ley, "Sexualität im Männer-KZ"; Glowacka, "Sexual Violence against Men and Boys"; see also Sommer, "Pipels"; Jones, "Bettmann"; Pollin-Gallay, *Occupied Words*, 143–64.
11 Wünschmann, *Before Auschwitz*; Knoll, "Es muss alles versucht werden," 237.
12 See, among others, Zinn, *Aus dem Volkskörper entfernt*; Brunner, *Als homosexuell verfolgt*.
13 Röll, "Homosexual Inmates"; Müller and Sternweiler, *Homosexuelle Männer*; Zinn, *"Das Glück kam immer zu mir"*; Ostrowska, Talewicz-Kwiatkowska, and Van Dijk, *Erinnern in Auschwitz*, 83–100; see also Mauthausen Memorial, "Queere Lagergeschichte(n)."
14 See, among others, Schoppmann, "Liebe wurde mit Prügelstrafe geahndet."
15 For various opinions on this question, see Penn, "Queer"; Schoppmann, "Eine Einleitung," in *Zeit der Maskierung*; Freedman, "The Burning of Letters Continues"; Carter, "Introduction: Theory, Methods, Praxis."
16 Many all-male concentration camps had brothels, but Jewish prisoners were not allowed to visit. Sommer, *Das KZ-Bordell*.
17 Janz, "Das Zeichen lesbisch."
18 See the differences between interwar Britain and Germany in Beachy, *Gay Berlin*; Doan, *Disturbing Practices*; and a summary discussion in Kunzel, "The Power of Queer History," 1564–6.
19 Evans, "Why Queer German History?"
20 Evans, "Why Queer German History?" 374; see also Kunzel, *Criminal Intimacy*.
21 The term "trans," similar to "queer," is a recent concept. Scholars have presented arguments for and against using it to describe persons from before the coinage of the term. See Stryker, *Transgender History*.
22 Volkov, "Antisemitism as a Cultural Code."
23 Pająk, "Echo Texts."
24 Heineman, "Sexuality and Nazism"; Herzog, *Sexuality in Europe*.
25 Eschebach, "Geschichte und Gedenken," 65. See also Schoppmann, *Nationalsozialistische Sexualpolitik*, 244–57; Janz, "Zeugnisse überlebender Frauen"; Gelbin, "Double Visions"; Rautenberg, *Homophobia in the Nazi Camps*.
26 Stephens, "Unhallowed Arts," 125–6.
27 Kuntsman, "Between Gulags and Pride Parades"; Healey, "Homophobia in Russia after 1945," in *Russian Homophobia*.
28 Beck, *Und Gad ging zu David*.
29 Dönhoff, *Ein gutes Leben*; Bochow and Pretzel, *Ich wollte es so normal*.
30 Frieda Belinfante, interview by Klaus Müller, 31 May 1994, USHMM, RG-50.030.0019; see also Boumans, *Een schitterend vergeten leven*.
31 Bondy, "Women in Theresienstadt"; Goldenberg and Shapiro, *Different Horrors*. This is also the case of Waxman's excellent *Women and the Holocaust*.

32 Sommer, "Pipels"; Glowacka, "Sexual Violence against Men and Boys"; Jones, "*Bettmann*"; see also the section on Nate Leipciger in chapter 2.
33 Jockusch, *Collect and Record!*; Garbarini, "Document Volumes"; Leff, *The Archive Thief*.
34 For the former: Herbert Nivelli, Wiener Holocaust Library [WL], III.h; for the latter: Laub, "Breaking the Silence."
35 For the former: Mühlhäuser, *Eroberungen*; Waxman, *Women and the Holocaust*; for the latter: Horowitz, "If He Knows to Make a Child."
36 University of South California Shoah Foundation Visual History Archive (hereafter VHA), Gad Beck Interview, #22791, 19 November 1996.
37 The following is a characterization based on my reading of our exchanges between 2010 and 2018.
38 Heger, *The Men with the Pink Triangle*. See also Tremblay, "Ich konnte ihren Schmerz körperlich spüren."
39 Hájková, "Aus Prag nach San Francisco."
40 There is a wealth of literature on invisible lesbian history; see among others Smith-Rosenberg, "The Female World."
41 Irene Miller Interview, 11 December 2002, *Jewish Family and Children's Services*, archived in VHA, #52553. There is an emergent scholarly work on the issues in keywording in the VHA and the biased history it produces: Cantillon, "Challenging the Shame Paradigm"; and Snyder, "Questions of Gender and Sexuality."
42 Irene Miller, interview by Christa Schikorra, April 1995, private archive of Christa Schikorra. Thanks to Christa for her immense generosity in drawing my attention to Miller, digitizing her oral history with Miller, sending it to me, and letting me publish about it.
43 On the role of a normative or clumsy interviewer, see Browning, *Remembering Survival*, Kindle locations 307–9, with thanks to Waitman Wade Beorn.
44 Pollak, *Grenzen des Sagbaren*; Langer, "Remembering Survival"; Jureit, *Erinnerungsmuster*; Greenspan, "The Unsaid"; Shenker, *Reframing Holocaust Testimony*.
45 See the powerful example discussed by Carli Snyder in Hájková, Krasuska, Strassfeld, Drinkwater, Gajowy, Yarfitz, Balling, and Snyder, "Queering Jewish Studies," 20.
46 For the context of these medical experiments, see Siegel, "Treating an Auschwitz Prisoner-Physician."
47 Sientje Backer, interview, 8 July 1997, USC VHA, # 32515.
48 On the transport, see Macadam, *999: The Extraordinary Young Women*. On queer women in Auschwitz, see Ostrowska, "Solche Berichte interessierten mich nie."
49 Linda Breder, *Jewish Survivor Linda Breder Testimony | USC Shoah Foundation*, interview by USC Shoah Foundation, 20 November 1996, USC VHA, #22979, www.youtube.com/watch?v=h_vlj-Mek0o; Cushman, "The Women of Birkenau," 286–93. Cushman's important book is forthcoming with Indiana University Press.

50 This point differs from my original German article, "Den Holocaust queer erzählen," 92–3. Cushman helpfully points out the positive light in which Breder described Schwalbová: Cushman, "The Women of Birkenau," 287–8.
51 Macadam, *999: The Extraordinary Young Women*, 357, where Edith Grossman, a fellow survivor, mentioned that Schwalbová was queer. Thanks to Denisa Nešťáková for alerting me to this and to Lisa Leff for sending me a copy of the page. In Schwalbová's memoir, there is no mention of her own queerness; Švalbová, *Vyhasnuté oči*.
52 Maja Suderland pointed out that survivors often depicted queer prisoners as deviant, but concrete individuals as friendly; see *Inside Concentration Camps*, 178.
53 Hart, *Fatal Women*; Mailänder, "Meshes of Power," 175–95.
54 Kraus and Kulka, *Death Factory*, 38.
55 Sommer, "Pipels."
56 Röll, "Homosexual Inmates"; Wachsmann, *KL: A History*, 503. For an exception, see Van Dijk, "In Auschwitz hatte ich meine größte Liebe," 60.
57 On the prisoner functionaries abusing teenage prisoners, see Ley, "Sexualität im Männer-KZ"; Glowacka, "Sexual Violence Against Men and Boys"; Sommer, "Pipels"; Jones, "*Bettmann*"; Ostrowska and van Dijk, "Pipels und Puppenjungen"; and the section on Leipciger in chapter 2.
58 Other authors pointed out this difference: Cushman, "The Women of Birkenau," 288, on Olga Lengyel.
59 Langbein, *People in Auschwitz*, 405.
60 There are two biographies of Langbein; neither thematizes his homophobia: Halbmayr, *Zeitlebens konsequent: Hermann Langbein*; Stengel, *Hermann Langbein*. The one scholar describing Langbein's moralizing and homophobia is Maja Suderland, *Inside Concentration Camps*, 181.
61 Dawidowicz, *The Holocaust and the Historians*, 8. Dawidowicz echoes the influential French author and Buchenwald survivor David Rousset, *A World Apart*, 35.
62 Johansson and Percy, "Homosexuals in Nazi Germany," Ch. 12, Part 1. See also the discussion in Tremblay, *A Badge of Injury*.
63 Pawełczynska, *Values and Violence in Auschwitz*, 98. Thanks to Doris Bergen for reminding me of this section. For a similar tone, see also Kogon, *Der SS-Staat*, 41, 268, 272.
64 Pawełczynska, *Values and Violence in Auschwitz*, 98; Kogon, *Der SS-Staat*, 41, 268, 272.
65 For a critical discussion of a similar analysis of "hard" and "situational" homosexuality, see Kunzel, "Situating Sex"; Samper Vendrell, *The Seduction of Youth*.
66 See also the discussion of lesbian prisoners following Krystyna Żywulska in Cesarani, *Final Solution*, 662.
67 Helm, *If This Is a Woman*, 174.
68 Helm, *If This Is a Woman*, 31.

69 Eschebach, "NS-Prozesse"; Erpel, *Im Gefolge der SS*; Kretzer, *NS-Täterschaft und Geschlecht*.
70 Helm, *If This Is a Woman*, 174.
71 Beck, *Und Gad ging zu David*; Beck, *An Underground Life*.
72 Frank Heibert, interview with the author, 18 June 2024.
73 The first edition of that book came out as Van Dijk, "*Ein erfülltes Leben*." Gad Beck's chapter is on pp. 100–13. The book is now in print as *Einsam war ich nie*.
74 The first interview is not publicly available, but I learned about it from my interviews with Claudia Schoppmann (18 June 2024) and Martina Voigt (21 June 2024); Gad Beck, interview by Klaus Müller, 16 February 1994, RG 50.030*0361, USHMM; VHA, 19 November 1996 and 7 April 1998, #22791.
75 Heibert, interview; information from the University of Wisconsin Press.
76 Heibert, interview; information from the University of Wisconsin Press.
77 Von der Heydt, "Wer fährt denn gerne." "Mischlinge," children of mixed marriages who were not members of the Jewish community, were not under threat of deportation.
78 See Müller, "Do You Remember, When." This exhibition is arranged alongside the scan of a Poesiealbum that Manfred Lewin dedicated to Beck.
79 For the history of Chug Chaluzi, see Rautenberg's 2008 thesis, *Zwischen Ideologie und Überleben*; and Rautenberg, "Zwischen Ideologie und Überleben."
80 Heibert, interview with the author, 10 June 2025.
81 "Our Friend Zvi," Pazzapazza, 15 March 2015, https://pazzapazza2.blogspot.com/2015/03/our-friend-zvi.html
82 Does and Cackett, *Die Freiheit des Erzählens*.
83 Does and Cackett, *Die Freiheit des Erzählens*.
84 Martina Voigt, interview with author, 20 June 2024. The movie *Die Freiheit des Erzählens* makes the same point.
85 Aviram, *Mit dem Mut der Verzweiflung*. Oskar Löwenstein did not publish a memoir, but in his oral history, he also does not mention a romantic or sexual relationship with Beck: VHA, 5 March 1996, #11178.
86 Aviram, *Mit dem Mut der Verzweiflung*, 109; Löwenstein VHA.
87 Carsten Does and Robin Cackett, interview with author, 29 October 2024.
88 *Die Freiheit des Erzählens*; Beck, *An Underground Life*, 84
89 Heibert, interview.
90 Interview with Löwenstein in Does and Cackett, *Die Freiheit des Erzählens*.
91 Heibert, interview. The second edition was the basis for the English translation. The German e-book is based on the first edition, and therefore the passage is in there.
92 Beck, *Und Gad ging zu David*, 68. There was an earlier book version, an advance copy for booksellers to attract book orders, that was more sexually explicit. Thanks to Frank Heibert for sharing his copy with me.
93 Bruns, *Politik des Eros*. See also Cleves, *Unspeakable*.
94 Heibert, interview.

95 Carsten Does and Robin Cackett, interview.
96 Rautenberg, "Homosexuality, Resistance and Aftermath." Thanks to Viola for sharing her paper with me.
97 Beck, *An Underground Life*, 118; Aviram, *Mit dem Mut der Verzweiflung*, 103–6.
98 Kosmala and Siegele, "Nachwort," in Aviram, *Mit dem Mut der Verzweiflung*, 209–23. It is worth noting that while the entire memoir is annotated showing painstaking research, the editors did not cite Lutz van Dijk's interview with Jizchak Schwersenz.
99 Beate Kosmala, message to the author, 25 June 2024. Patrick Siegele did not give permission for his response to be cited. Ostrowska, *Jene: Homosexuelle während des Zweiten Weltkriegs*.
100 I am grateful for the input of the participants in the USHMM Jack and Anita Hess Faculty Seminar, "LGBTQ+ Histories of the Holocaust," 4–8 January 2021. See also *Die Freiheit des Erzählens*.
101 Beck, *An Underground Life*, 39. In the documentary *Die Freiheit des Erzählens*, Beck described this moment "as not so bad." Echoing the discussion below, the interviewer suggested it was sexual abuse or rape, to which Beck responded "I did not use this word at all, you see, I thought, he too has the right [to have sex]. And it was not that unpleasant."
102 Beck, *An Underground Life*, 119.
103 Voigt, interview.
104 Yizkor bukh Jizchak Schwersenz, 1944, Lochamei Haghettaot, 28627. Thanks to Viola Alianov Rautenberg for telling me where to find the document, and to Greta Barak for sending me a scan.
105 Joachim S., "Für meinen jungen Freund alles riskiert," in Van Dijk, *Einsam war ich nie*, 92.
106 Schwersenz, *Die versteckte Gruppe*, 137.
107 Both the letter in Van Dijk, as well as the way Schwersenz wrote about Chones, portray the two as seeing each other as pupil and teacher.
108 Joachim S., "Für meinen jungen Freund alles riskiert," in Van Dijk, *Einsam war ich nie*, 95.
109 Bruns, *Politik des Eros*. See also discussion later in this chapter regarding Fredy Hirsch.
110 Hájková, "Sexual Barter in Times of Genocide."
111 Does and Cackett, *Die Freiheit des Erzählens*, 1:26, translation mine.
112 Carsten Does and Robin Cackett, interview. See also Rheinberg and Dittrich, *Jahresbericht 2000*.
113 Hájková, *The Last Ghetto*.
114 Entry for 10 September 1944, in Redlich, *Zítra jedeme*. This entry is missing in both the Hebrew and English editions: Bondy, *As-If Living*; Friedman, *The Terezin Diary of Gonda Redlich*. Thanks to Nir Cohen and Amos Goldberg for translating the Hebrew original for me, which is kept in the Archive of the Jewish Museum in Prague, Terezín, 324a.
115 Redlich, *Zítra jedeme*, entry for 15 June 1943, 195. This entry is present in the Hebrew and English translation.

116 Bondy also censored other passages that could have made Redlich unpalatable to the modern public or made the Terezín prisoner community not suitably Jewish for Israeli readers. See Hájková, *The Last Ghetto*, 1–2.
117 Bondy, "Women in Theresienstadt," 320, 326. The footnote on p. 326 should be 47 but is printed as 46. Bondy cited here the 1943 Redlich entry on queer girl teenagers.
118 Diary of Ralph Oppenhejm, entry for 24 March 1945, Jewish Danish Museum, 207 A 35, 7. Oppenhejm's diary is not to be confused with his biographically influenced novel, *An der Grenze des Lebens*. Thanks to Silvia Goldbaum Tarabini for drawing my attention to the passage and for translating it for me, as she did all other citations from Danish.
119 For the history of gay male friendship with heterosexual women, see Portmann, *Women and Gay Men*, and also Bengry's review of this book in *Gender & History*. Bengry helpfully points out the tradition of gay male misogyny vis-à-vis their women friends, which is a frequent occurrence in Oppenhejm's diary. See for instance the entry for 7 April 1945.
120 Marhoefer, "Lesbianism, Transvestitism, and the Nazi State."
121 Ellen Oppenhejm, interview with the author, January 2010; Ellen Oppenhejm, interviews with Silvia Goldbaum Tarabini, various dates, archive of Silvia Goldbaum Tarabini.
122 In contrast to my original article in German, "Holocaust queer erzählen," 95, I was able to ascertain that Julie Fleischerová was not identical to Marianne because Fleischerová was mentioned by name in a neighbouring entry. With thanks to Tomáš Fedorovič for help.
123 Hájková, "Die fabelhaften Jungs."
124 Fall, *Terezín, ráj mezi lágry*, 36.
125 Hájková, *The Last Ghetto*, 49–50.
126 On Mosse, see Meyer, "Chapter 2 – Walking on a Thin Line: The Participation of the Reichsvereinigung and the Berlin Jewish Community during the Deportations," in *A Fatal Balancing Act*; Samper Vendrell, "The Case of a German-Jewish Lesbian Woman."
127 Ondřichová, *Příběh Fredyho Hirsche*, 13–15.
128 Police directorate in Brno to the Regional authority, 3 September 1937, Moravian Regional Archive Brno, Regional office Brno, III. manipulace, box 2280, #34492; Mikovcová, "Brněnské období Fredyho Hirsche." I am grateful to Dr. Mikovcová for drawing my attention to this source.
129 See also Hájková, *The Last Ghetto*, 87.
130 Some historians discuss Hirsch's eminent role while erasing his queerness: Kwiet and Eschwege, *Selbstbehauptung und Widerstand*, 291–3.
131 Ondřichová, *Příběh Fredyho Hirsche*, 64–5, citing Irma Lauscherová, one of the youth care workers.
132 Kárný, "Fragen zum 8. März 1944."
133 Ondřichová, *Příběh Freddyho Hirsche*, 35.
134 Hájková, "Fredy Hirsch's Lover." Almost none of the Hirsch biographers mention Mautner's existence, with the exception of Gat, *Freddy HaYakar*.
135 Interview of a man born 1926, 1 April 1995, Jewish Museum Prague (hereafter AJMP), interviews, #645.

136 Ondřichová, *Příběh Fredyho Hirsche*, 64–5.
137 Ondřichová, *Příběh Fredyho Hirsche*, 15, citing Irma Lauscherová.
138 Interview of a woman born 1926, 13 February 1995, AJMP, The Oral History Collection, #407.
139 Ondřichová, *Příběh Fredyho Hirsche*, 65, 71.
140 Interview of Tomáš Fantl, 30 August 1995, AJMP, The Oral History Collection, 482.
141 With the important exception of Ondřichová, none of the biographies, be they books or documentaries, address these accusations: Kämper, *Fredy Hirsch*; Sommerová, "Krotitel esesáků"; Gat, *Freddy HaYakar*; Růžička, "Fredy. Hagibor. Hrdina."
142 Brom, "Giora Manor."
143 Hájková, "A Society Based on Inequality," in *The Last Ghetto*.
144 Karl Gorath from Bremerhaven is one of the best-known survivors with a pink triangle but it is never mentioned that he had criminal records for both §175 and §176 (sex with minors). For criticism of the lack of courage to face these difficult histories, see Evans, "The Optics of Desire," in *The Queer Art of History*, and the exhibition in the Schwules Museum, Berlin: Bosold, Rappe-Weber, Heim, and Woltersdorff, *Aufarbeiten*.
145 Bruns, *Politik des Eros*, 242–5; Dudek, "Exkurs: Eros und Knabenliebe."
146 See also Stryker, *Transgender History*, 22–4. For more context of writing trans history, see among others, LaFleur, Raskolnikov, and Kłosowska, *Trans Historical*.
147 On trans Jewish history, see among others, Rachamimov, "From Lesbian Radicalism"; Wolfert, *Charlotte Charlaque*; Strassfeld, *Trans Talmud*; Hájková, Krasuska, Strassfeld, Drinkwater, Gajowy, Yarfitz, Balling, and Snyder, "Queering Jewish Studies." See also Korbel, "Portrayals of a Female Impersonator."
148 Herrn, "Transvestitismus in der NS-Zeit." See also Dobler, "Damen-und Herrenimitator_innen."
149 Marhoefer, "Transgender Life"; Ashton, "The Parallel Lives"; see also Nunn, "Trans Liminality."
150 Bloomfield, *Drag: A British History*, 5.
151 Bloomfield, *Drag: A British History*, 5; Stryker, *Transgender History*, 22–4.
152 Sutton, *Sexuality in Modern German History*, 54.
153 CV for Harry Heymann-Hambo, minutes of the Council of Elders for March 1945, National Archive Prague, KT OVS, inv. nr. 64, box 45, file 29.
154 For Hambo's biographical information, see their reparation file at the Entschädigungsamt Berlin, #67710. Thanks to Maria von der Heydt for copying the file for me.
155 Fracapane, *The Jews of Denmark*, 156.
156 Oppenhejm, entry for 6 April 1944, Danish Jewish Museum, 207 A 35, 7.
157 Lustig, "Moral Education," in *Night and Hope*; Fracapane, *The Jews of Denmark*, 156, 167.
158 Fracapane, *The Jews of Denmark*, 156.
159 On Leský, see Melamed, *They Shall Be Counted*; Makarova, *Closer to the Truth*.

160 Leo Säbel, interview by Silvia Goldbaum Tarabini. Thanks to Silvia for sharing this information.
161 Hájková, "Har du information om Hambo?" With thanks to Silvia Goldbaum Tarabini and Bent Blüdnikow.
162 Kassow, *Who Will Write Our History?*
163 Spivak, "Can the Subaltern Speak?," 297. I am grateful to Elissa Mailänder for pointing this out to me.
164 Kunzel, "The Power of Queer History."

2. People without History Are Dust

1 Nestle, "Review: Into the Mainstream"; see also Nestle, "The Kiss, 1950s–1990s." See also Nestle, email to author, 12 November 2017.
2 See also Funke, "The World."
3 Pająk, "Echo Texts," 11–34.
4 See also Karczewski, "Transnational Flows of Knowledge."
5 Doan, "Queer History/Queer Memory"; Lochrie, "Have We Ever Been Normal?"
6 On queer readings, see among others, Evans, "Why Queer German History?" On queer kinship, see also Evans, "Sound, Listening and the Queer Art of History."
7 Langer, *Admitting the Holocaust*, 46; for a critical discussion, see Adler, "Hrubieszów at the Crossroads."
8 Beachy, *Gay Berlin*.
9 See chapter 1.
10 Evans, "Why Queer German History?" 374; Hájková, "Introduction: Sexuality, Holocaust, Stigma," 10.
11 Beachey, *Gay Berlin*; Doan, *Disturbing Practices*.
12 The following is taken from my interview with Margot Heuman, 5–9 April 2018; Interview Margot Heuman, 2 December 1994, VHA; Interview Margot Heuman, 31 July 1992, USHMM, RG 50.233.0054.
13 Margot Heuman, interview with the author, 5–9 April 2018.
14 Meyer, *A Fatal Balancing Act*, 246.
15 On Theresienstadt, see Hájková, *The Last Ghetto*.
16 The address today is Náměstí ČSA 216.
17 She stated as much to the JOINT, International Tracing Service Arolsen, as one of five desired destinations; see Ordner DP1455, Namen von HETMAN, MARGARETA bis HEWYK, Demian (2), Arolsen Archives, https://collections.arolsen-archives.org/de/document/67354089.
18 "Diviš Václav & Divišová Karla," *Yad Vashem*.
19 As this person never publicly acknowledged the relationship, I do not cite the memoir to preserve their anonymity. For another mention of romantic attraction between girls in a Theresienstadt youth home, see Redlich, *Zítra jedeme*, entry for 15 June 1943, 195.
20 See, for example, Robinson, "Opera Queen."
21 See Kárný, "Terezínský rodinný tabor."
22 Archive of the State Museum Stutthof, Einlieferungsbuch, sign. I-IIE-11. With thanks to Dr. Danuta Drywa.

23. Ellger, "Hamburg Neugraben."
24. Margot Heuman, interview with author. On this coerced relationship, see Hájková, "Between Love and Coercion."
25. Chauncey, *Gay New York*.
26. Unfortunately, neither Margot nor her son remember Lissy's last name. On the history of the domestic labour of Black women, see Walters, "Overview: The History of Black Women's Domestic Labor," 13–26.
27. Gutterman, *Her Neighbor's Wife*.
28. Margot Heuman Interview, USHMM.
29. See also Carli Snyder in Hájková, Krasuska, Strassfeld, Drinkwater, Gajowy, Yarfitz, Balling, and Snyder, "Queering Jewish Studies"; see also the first chapter in this volume.
30. Margot Heuman, interview with Richmond in *Surviving Together*.
31. Hájková, "Queer Desire in the Holocaust: I Did Not Want to Die."
32. Green, "Margot Heuman."
33. Weston, *Families We Choose*; Eng, *The Feeling of Kinship*.
34. Butler, "Is Kinship Always Already Heterosexual?"
35. Berlant, "Intimacy," 285.
36. Berlant, "Intimacy," 286.
37. See also Overing, Fortis, and Margiotti, "Kinship in Anthropology."
38. See, for example, Lower, *The Ravine*; cf. Walke, "Review of *The Ravine*."
39. Milton, "Women and the Holocaust."
40. Hájková, "A Society Based on Inequality" and "Medicine and Illness," in *The Last Ghetto*; Walke, "Fighting for Life and Victory: Refugees from the Ghettos and the Soviet Partisan Movement" and "Of Refuge and Resistance: Labor for Survival in the 'Zorin Family Unit,'" in *Pioneers and Partisans*.
41. On this point, see also Evans, "Sound, Listening and the Queer Art of History"; Nemerofsky Ramsay, *The Muranów Lily*. See also Evans, *Queer Art of History*, 5–6.
42. Cook, "Families of Choice?"; Evans, "Listening for Queer Kinship"; Evans, *The Queer Art of History*.
43. See also Hájková, *The Last Ghetto*; Bourdeau, "I Am Jeopardizing Everyone."
44. Margot Heuman, interview with the author.
45. Leipciger, *Weight of Freedom*; see also Glowacka, "Sexual Violence against Men and Boys"; Dwork, "Sexual Abuse."
46. Sawicka, "Fünfteichen"; see also Sawicka, "Fünfteichen (Miłoszyce koło Wrocławia)."
47. I reached out to Gross Rosen Memorial to ascertain Janek's identity but unfortunately that was not possible. Leokadia Lewandowska from Gross Rosen Memorial, email to the author, 5 December 2023.
48. See Sommer, "Pipels," 86–103; Ostrowska and van Dijk, "Pipels und Puppenjungen," 113–26.
49. Jones, "*Bettmann*."
50. Leipciger, *Weight of Freedom*, 92.
51. Leipciger, *Weight of Freedom*, 92.
52. Leipciger, *Weight of Freedom*, 92–3.

53 Jones, "*Bettmann.*"
54 Leipciger, *Weight of Freedom*, 93.
55 Leipciger, *Weight of Freedom*, 93.
56 Hájková, "Sexual Barter in Times of Genocide."
57 Dwork, "Sexual Abuse"; Leipciger, *Weight of Freedom*, xxv.
58 Leipciger, *Weight of Freedom*, xxv.
59 On that point, see also Sliwa, *Jewish Childhood in Kraków*.
60 Thus, the pithy summary of Reviewer 1, whom I thank for pushing me here.
61 Ilse van Liempt's analysis of free consent and sex trafficking is useful here: "Trafficking in Human Beings"; see also Hájková, "Why We Need a History of Prostitution."
62 Glowacka noted how difficult it was for Leipciger to share this story: Glowacka, "Sexual Violence against Men and Boys," 93.
63 Leipciger, *Weight of Freedom*, 93.
64 Leipciger, *Weight of Freedom*, 260.
65 Glowacka, "Sexual Violence against Men and Boys," 85.
66 Mikel Arieli, "Reading *The Diary of Anne Frank*."
67 McGrane, "Fight Over Anne Frank's Fallen Tree"; "Anne Frank overleed eerder" (with thanks to Anne Gerritsen, who pointed me towards this article).
68 Sullivan, *The Betrayal of Anne Frank*.
69 Franklin, "Beyond the Betrayal"; Van der Boom and Vastenhout, "Réfutation du livre *The Betrayal of Anne Frank*."
70 With important exceptions: Ellenzweig, "Anne Frank: The Secret Annex"; Elman, "Lesbians and the Holocaust," 14–15; Hann, "If only I had a girlfriend!." Ruth Franklin's book unfortunately operates with hard sexual identity (as opposed to queerness): Franklin, *The Many Lives of Anne Frank*, 105–28.
71 Jackman, "Anne Frank Was Attracted to Girls"; Jackman built on Rachel Watkins's tweet (@rwatkinsphoto, Twitter, 6 September 2017); Gerber, "As a Queer Jew." A radical lesbian fanzine by the name of *Anne FranQ* appeared in Tel Aviv at the beginning of the 2000s. My thanks to Yossi Bartal for this information.
72 6 January 1944 entry in Frank, *Anne Frank: The Collected Works*, 548. On the transmission of the text: Anne Frank wrote the first version of the diary, Version A, which contains the above cited entry. In 1944, she began a revision for later publication, Version B, in which the entry was removed. Version C is the publication chosen by Otto Frank (see below). I have worked with the text in the original, accessible via scan: https://annefrankmanuscripten.org/nl/manuscripten/dagboek/2-094.
73 Hann, "If only I had a girlfriend!," 15.
74 I would briefly like to note that I in no way wish to endorse Ellenzweig's somewhat sexist terminology. Ellenzweig, "The Secret Annex," 45.
75 20 June 1942 entry in Anne Frank, *Anne Frank: The Collected Works*.
76 Hann, "If only I had a girlfriend!," 19–20. She is discussing the entry from 18 March 1944 in *Anne Frank Gesamtausgabe*, 180–1 and 640–1. See also "A Holocaust Survivor's Frank Story."
77 Müller, *Anne Frank: The Biography*, 349.

78 Lebovic, "Who was Anne Frank's Gay Uncle Walter?"
79 Lebovic, "Who was Anne Frank's Gay Uncle Walter?"
80 Disappointingly, this is the only reading Ruth Franklin offers; Franklin, *The Many Lives of Anne Frank*, 116–20.
81 Hann, "If only I had a girlfriend!," 8–9.
82 Barnouw, *The Phenomenon of Anne Frank*, 20–1.
83 Barnouw, *The Phenomenon of Anne Frank*, 21; see also 27.
84 Folman and Polonsky, *Anne Frank's Diary*, 90–1.
85 Harris and Alter, "With Rising Book Bans."
86 Andrew Lapin, interview with author, 19 October 2023.
87 Lapin, "Meet Bruce Friedman."
88 "CS/CS/HB 1069: Education."
89 Lapin, "Anne Frank's Diary."
90 Closson, "Major Publishers Sue Florida." As of June 2025, there was no ruling.
91 Lapin, interview.
92 Shainmain, "Anne Frank's Diary: The Graphic Adaptation."
93 David Barnouw, email to the author, 15 January 2021. With thanks to David Barnouw for his permission to cite our correspondence.
94 Van Maarsen, *My Name Is Anne*, 94. I should note here that "queer" is used as an abbreviation above; Van Maarsen would probably not have known the term.
95 Van Maarsen, *My Name Is Anne*.
96 "A Holocaust Survivor's Frank Story."
97 On epistemological injustice, see Hann, "If only I had a girlfriend!," 31–4, which in turn was built on Fricker, *Epistemic Injustice*. See also chapter 1 of this book.
98 Rich, "Compulsory Heterosexuality."
99 Lapin, interview.
100 Applebaum, *Buried Words*. I would like to thank Dagmar Herzog for telling me of the existence of this diary.
101 After the war, Melania Weissenberg emigrated to Canada where she changed her first name to Molly and after marrying took the last name Applebaum. I refer to her as Molly Applebaum, because that is the name under which her diary is known.
102 Jan Grabowski, Introduction to Applebaum, *Buried Words*, xviii; See also Crisci, "Dąbrowa Tarnowska."
103 Among others, see Timm, "The Challenges of Including Sexual Violence," 358.
104 Applebaum, *Buried Words*, 13 April 1942, entry 4.
105 Maynes, "Age as a Category"; Sköld and Söderlind, "Agentic Subjects"; Gleason, "Avoiding the Agency Trap." For Holocaust history and Krakow, see Sliwa, *Jewish Childhood*. With thanks to Hannah J. Elizabeth for the advice.
106 Sabina Goldman to Melania Weissenberg, 11 September 1942, quoted in Applebaum, *Buried Words*, 63.
107 Applebaum, *Buried Words*, 11n13.

108 Applebaum, *Buried Words*, Entries for 9 September 1942 and 28 September 1942 ("the creature I love the most in the world"), 8 and 11; Entry for 22 February 1943 (last entry to Sabina).
109 These photos are held by the United States Holocaust Memorial Museum, inventor nr. 2016.442.1, https://collections.ushmm.org/search/catalog/irn551471#?rsc=167746&cv=12&c=0&m=0&s=0&xywh=0%2C-43%2C1256%2C1076. Translation by the author with thanks to Katarzyna Person and Maria von der Heydt.
110 Applebaum, *Buried Words*; Molly's Memoir, 43–117, 64.
111 Applebaum, *Buried Words*, 54, 63.
112 Applebaum, *Buried Words*, 102.
113 Applebaum, *Buried Words*, 111–13.
114 Applebaum, *Buried Words*, 109–13.
115 Grabowski, Introduction to Applebaum, *Buried Words*, xxiii. The special issue of *Holocaust Studies* on Applebaum's diary edited by Stephanie Corazza did not address the queer aspects of the diary: Corazza, "Introduction to Buried Words."
116 Horowitz, "What We Learn, at Last," 56. Horowitz here writes that the diary could be read in such a way that Molly was also attracted to Helena, the cousin who was with her in hiding.
117 In my opinion, the minutes of his conversation with the secret police are too problematic to be used as a source. See also Tomek, "Svazek StB jako historický pramen," 210.
118 Interview of a man born 1926, AJMP, 5 February 2007, The Oral History Collection, interview nr. 1089.
119 Pavlát, "Propagátor české židovské kultury Jiří Vrba."
120 In August 2018, as I was reading through the Vrba collection, I signed the contract with Oxford University Press.
121 Edward Serotta, interview with author, 2 November 2024.
122 For both memories of Eva Kominíková, one page note, collection Vrba, AJMP, 16.
123 Oral History Eva Krušinová, Visual History Archive, 26 February 1996, #11399.
124 See Hájková, "Medicine and Illness," in *The Last Ghetto*.
125 See Ondřichová, *Příběh Fredyho Hirsche*; Hájková, "Fredy Hirsch's Lover."
126 Testimony of Jiří Vrba, Archive of the Terezín Memorial (hereafter APT), testimonies, 2238, recorded 3 October 1988.
127 Eva Kominíková-Gottwaldová, "Jak vzpomínám na Jirku Vrbu," 27 February 1995, collection Vrba, AJMP.
128 Testimony of Jiří Vrba, APT.
129 Kominíková-Gottwaldová, "Jak vzpomínám na Jirku Vrbu"; Vrba's handwritten program note, collection Vrba, AŽMP.
130 Anamnestický dotazník, no date (1980); Psychologické vyšetření, collection Hlavní správa rozvědky SNB – svazky (I. S): reg. č. 12484/306 I. S*, Security Services Archive (hereafter ABS).
131 Testimony of Jiří Vrba, APT; Miroslav Kárný, "Částečný seznam soudruhů a soudružek, kteří v letech 1941–1945 pracovali v ilegální organizaci

KSČ v terezínském koncentračním táboře," in Kárný, "Komunistická organizace v terezínském koncentračním táboře 1941–1945" (manuscript, 1983), Czech National Archive, Kárných, ka 16, 7–10. See also Hájková, *The Last Ghetto*, 89.
132 Anamnestický dotazník, undated (1980). Richard Kraus (1887–1942) was the cousin of Adolf Vrba, Jiří's father.
133 Kraus's documents in Arolsen Archives; Jaroslav Želivský (= Jaroslav Hošek), Seznam všech interbrigadistů, NA Prague, SPB, 2209.
134 Testimony of Jiří Vrba, APT; see also Kosta, *Život mezi úzkostí a nadějí*.
135 Testimony of Jiří Vrba, APT.
136 Testimony of Jiří Vrba, APT.
137 See the section on Margot Heuman in this book.
138 On the fate of these transports, see Flusser, *Život na úvěr*, 57–162; on Blechhammer, see Piper, "Blechhammer."
139 Interview with Miroslav Spořitel (pseudonym), 16 November 2018.
140 Edward Serotta, interview; Adolf Vrba's prisoner card from Buchenwald, ITS Arolsen, https://collections.arolsen-archives.org/de/search/person/7354580?s=adolf%20vrba%201893&t=1822711&p=0.
141 Robert Y. Büchler, "Kinderblock 66 im KL Buchenwald," archive of the Buchenwald Memorial, 31/666, 7. The text is Büchler's own translation from the Hebrew original of his piece from Moreshet 1978.
142 We only have Spořitel's word for this story. I have checked in his records in Brno, where he moved on 11 July 1945, and as his last address he gave Buchenwald. This date does not exclude a trip to Paris, but many Czech Buchenwald survivors returned only in mid-July. Vrba's police registration file, Z 1 – Sbírka pobytové evidence občanů, Brno (1909, 1918–1953), Nová evidence; Brno municipal archive. With thanks to Hana Skopalová.
143 Testimony of Jiří Vrba, APT.
144 Adelheid and Gerhard Frey Reinininghaus, "Schritte auf unserem Weg mit Jiří Vrba," collection Vrba, AJMP.
145 Oral History Eva Krušinová, VHA.
146 CV Vrba, collection Vrba, AJMP.
147 Jiří Suchý, "V Semaforu," collection Vrba, AJMP.
148 Zuzana Lejčarová, interview with author, 26 July 2022.
149 Zuzana Lejčarová, interview.
150 Zuzana Lejčarová, interview.
151 Jan Krušina, interview with author, 27 July 2022.
152 There is not much literature in English on the StB, but see Williams and Deletant, "Czechoslovakia 1990–2," in *Security Intelligence Services*, 55–82.
153 Souhrn, fond Hlavní správa rozvědky SNB – svazky (I. S): reg. č. 12484/306 I. S*, ABS.
154 Seidl, Wintr, and Nozar, *Od žaláře k oltáři*, 273–95.
155 Potužil, interview, *Paměť národa*; Bloudek, interview, *Paměť národa*; Špaček, *Člověk byl snadno vydíratelný*.
156 On Kárný, see Tesař, "Miroslav Kárný"; Hallama, "A Great Civic and Scientific Duty."

157 Brod, interview, *Paměť národa*.
158 Beruna Kopoldová, interview with author, 25 July 2022.
159 The secret police planned to send Vrba to Sweden to spy on the emigré politician Zdeněk Hejzlar, but it did not come to pass. Věc: návrh pro uložení podsvazku, signed Čeřil, 11. června 1985, Hlavní správa rozvědky SNB – svazky (I. S): reg. č. 12484/306 I. S*, (ABS).
160 Testimonies of Reininghaus, Karin Meyer, Milan Schulz, Kopoldová, all in collection Vrba, AJMP.
161 Memorandum, 22 July 1981, Hlavní správa rozvědky SNB – svazky (I. S): reg. č. 12484/306 I. S*, (ABS).
162 Miroslav Spořitel, interview.
163 Miloš Bondy (Povondra), "Co odvál dým," 193, 196, AJMP. He says here that this Vrba was from Brno; however, Jiří Vrba was the only prisoner with that name in Buchenwald. Possibly, Povondra mixed up Vrba's place of background with the city to which he ended up moving after liberation.
164 Edward Serotta, interview with author.
165 Frommer, *National Cleansing*; Fitzpatrick, "Signals from Below."
166 I should like to thank Adam Drda for this assessment. Further information about Vrba's activities comes from my interview with Vrba's nephew, Jan Krusina, from 27 July 2022.
167 Testimony of Jiří Vrba, APT, Michaela Vidláková, "Štafetový běžec," (1994), collection Vrba, AJMP.
168 Martin Šmok, email and phone call to the author, 5 September 2022.
169 Obituary notice Vrba, collection Vrba, AJMP.
170 Edward Serotta, interview.
171 Serotta, *Out of the Shadows*, 52–3, 254.
172 Serotta, *Out of the Shadows*, 63, 75.
173 Edward Serotta, interview.
174 Centropa, "Preserving Jewish Memory."
175 Doan, "Queer History/Queer Memory," 121.
176 Horowitz, "What We Learn, at Last."
177 Hann, "If only I had a girlfriend!," 31–2.
178 Hann, "If only I had a girlfriend!," 31–2.
179 See the first chapter in this volume.
180 Here, I am building on the idea of "difficult history." On this, see Rose, *Interpreting Difficult History*; Evans, "Sound, Listening and the Queer Art of History," 40.
181 Funke, "The World"; Marhoefer, *Racism and the Making of Gay Rights*; Evans, *Queer Art of History*; and many others.

Bibliography

Adler, Eliyana R. "Hrubieszów at the Crossroads: Polish Jews Navigate the German and Soviet Occupations." *Holocaust and Genocide Studies* 28, no. 1 (Spring 2014): 1–30. https://doi.org/10.1093/hgs/dcu010.

"Anne Frank overleed eerder dan werd aangenomen." *De Trouw*, 31 March 2015. https://www.trouw.nl/nieuws/anne-frank-overleed-eerder-dan-werd-aangenomen~beec0f8f/.

Applebaum, Molly. *Buried Words: The Diary of Molly Applebaum*. Toronto: Azrieli Foundation, 2017.

Arend, Sabine, and Petra Fank, eds. *Ravensbrück denken: Gedenk- und Erinnerungskultur im Spannungsfeld von Gegenwart und Zukunft*. Berlin: Metropol, 2020.

Ashton, Bodie A. "The Parallel Lives of Liddy Bacroff: Transgender (Pre)History and the Tyranny of the Archive in Twentieth-Century Germany." *German History* 42, no. 1 (March 2024): 79–100. https://doi.org/10.1093/gerhis/ghad071.

Aviram, Zvi. *Mit dem Mut der Verzweiflung: mein Widerstand im Berliner Untergrund 1943–1945*, edited by Beate Kosmala and Patrick Siegele. Berlin: Metropol, 2015.

Barnouw, David. *The Phenomenon of Anne Frank*. Bloomington: Indiana University Press, 2018. https://doi.org/10.2307/j.ctt21215t3.

Beachy, Robert. *Gay Berlin: Birthplace of a Modern Identity.* New York: Knopf, 2014.

Beck, Gad. *An Underground Life: Memoirs of a Gay Jew in Nazi Berlin,* edited by Frank Heibert. Translated by Allison Brown. Madison: University of Wisconsin Press, 1999.

– *Und Gad ging zu David: Die Erinnerungen des Gad Beck 1923 bis 1945,* edited by Frank Heibert. Berlin: Edition diá, 1995.

Bengry, Justin. "Review of John Portmann, *Women and Gay Men in the Postwar Period.*" *Gender & History* 29, no. 2 (August 2017): 468–9. https://doi.org/10.1111/1468-0424.12299.

Berlant, Laurent. "Intimacy: A Special Issue." *Critical Inquiry* 24, no. 2 (Winter 1998): 281–8. https://doi.org/10.1086/448875.

Bloomfield, Jacob. *Drag: A British History.* Berkeley: University of California Press, 2023. https://doi.org/10.1525/9780520393332.

Bochow, Michael, and Andreas Pretzel, eds. *Ich wollte es so normal wie andere auch: Walter Guttmann erzählt sein Leben.* Hamburg: Männerschwarm, 2011.

Bondy, Ruth, ed. *As-If Living: A Diary of Egon Redlich from Theresienstadt Ghetto (1942–1944).* Lohamei Hagetaot: Hakibbutz Hameuchad Publishing and Beit Lohamei Hagetaot, 1982.

– "Women in Theresienstadt and the Family Camp in Birkenau." In *Women in the Holocaust,* edited by Dalia Ofer and Lenore Weitzman, 310–26. New Haven, NJ: Yale University Press, 1998.

Bosold, Birgit, Susanne Rappe-Weber, Tino Heim, and Volker Woltersdorff, curs. *Aufarbeiten: Sexualisierte Gewalt gegen Kinder und Jugendliche im Zeichen von Emanzipation.* Exhibition at the Schwules Museum, Berlin, 2023.

Boumans, Toni. *Een schitterend vergeten leven: de eeuw van Frieda Belinfante.* Amsterdam: Balans, 2016.

Brom, Dotan. "Giora Manor, the Kibbutz and the Transparent Closet." In *Queer Jewish Lives between Central Europe and Mandatory Palestine: Biographies and Geographies,* edited by Andreas Kraß, Moshe Sluhovsky, and Yuval Yonay, 291–310. Bielefeld: Transcript, 2021. https://doi.org/10.1515/9783839453322.

Browning, Christopher R. *Remembering Survival: Inside a Nazi Slave-Labor Camp.* New York: W.W. Norton, 2010. Kindle.

Brunner, Andreas. *Als homosexuell verfolgt: Wiener Biografien aus der NS-Zeit.* Vienna: Mandelbaum, 2023.

Bruns, Claudia. *Politik des Eros: Der Männerbund in Wissenschaft, Politik und Jugendkultur (1880–1934)*. Cologne: Böhlau, 2008.

Butler, Judith. "Is Kinship Always Already Heterosexual?" *Differences* 13, no. 1 (May 2002): 14–44. https://doi.org/10.1215/10407391-13-1-14.

Carter, Julian B. "Introduction: Theory, Methods, Praxis: The History of Sexuality and the Question of Evidence." *Journal of the History of Sexuality* 14, nos. 1–2 (January–April 2005): 1–9. https://doi.org/10.1353/sex.2006.0005.

Cesarani, David. *Final Solution: The Fate of the Jews 1933–1949*. London: Macmillan, 2015.

Chauncey, George. *Gay New York: Gender, Urban Culture, and the Making of the Gay Male World, 1890–1940*. New York: Basic Books, 1995.

Cleves, Rachel Hope. *Unspeakable: A Life beyond Sexual Morality*. Chicago: University of Chicago Press, 2020. https://doi.org/10.7208/chicago/9780226733678.001.0001.

Closson, Troy. "Major Publishers Sue Florida over Banned School Library Books." *New York Times*, August 29, 2024. https://www.nytimes.com/2024/08/29/us/florida-book-ban-lawsuit.html.

Cook, Matt. "Families of Choice? George Ives, Queer Lives and the Family in Early Twentieth-Century Britain." *Gender & History* 22, no. 1 (April 2010): 1–20. https://doi.org/10.1111/j.1468-0424.2009.01575.x.

Corazza, Stephanie. "Introduction to Buried Words: Sexuality, Violence and Holocaust Testimonies." *Holocaust Studies* 27, no. 4 (2021): 441–6. https://doi.org/10.1080/17504902.2021.1894019.

Crenshaw, Kimberlé. "Mapping the Margins." In *Critical Race Theory: The Key Writings That Formed the Movement*, edited by Kimberlé Crenshaw, Neil Gotanda, Gary Peller, and Kendall Thomas, 357–83. New York: The New Press, 1995.

Crisci, Caterina. "Dąbrowa Tarnowska." In *Encyclopedia of Camps and Ghettos, 1933–1945, Vol. 2, A: Ghettos in German-Occupied Eastern Europe*, edited by Martin Dean, 496–8. Bloomington: Indiana University Press, 2012. https://doi.org/10.1353/document.2635.

Cushman, Sarah. "The Women of Birkenau." PhD diss., Clark University, 2010.

Dawidowicz, Lucy S. *The Holocaust and the Historians*. Cambridge, MA: Harvard University Press, 1981.

Doan, Laura. *Disturbing Practices: History, Sexuality, and Women's Experience of Modern War*. Chicago: University of Chicago Press, 2013. https://doi.org/10.7208/chicago/9780226001753.001.0001.

- "Queer History/Queer Memory: The Case of Alan Turing." *GLQ* 23, no. 1 (January 2017): 113–36. https://muse.jhu.edu/article/645206.
Dobler, Jens. "Damen-und Herrenimitator_innen 1870–1933. Travestie zwischen Beruf, Berufung und Bewegung." In *Communities, Camp und Camouflage: Bewegung in Kunst und Kultur*, edited by Carolin Küppers and Rainer Marbach, 42–9. Hamburg: Männerschwarm, 2017.
Dönhoff, Friedrich. *Ein gutes Leben ist die beste Antwort: Die Geschichte des Jerry Rosenstein*. Zurich: Diogenes, 2014.
Dudek, Peter. *"Sie sind und bleiben eben die alte abstrakte Ideologe!" Der Reformpädagoge Gustav Wyneken (1875–1864) – Eine Biographie*. Bad Heilbrunn: Julius Klinkhardt, 2017.
Dwork, Debórah. "Sexual Abuse, Sexual Barter, and Silence." *Holocaust Studies* 27, no. 4 (2021): 495–500. https://doi.org/10.1080/17504902.2021.1893300.
Ellenzweig, Allen. "Anne Frank: The Secret Annex and the Closet." *Response: A Contemporary Jewish Review* 67 (Winter/Spring 1997): 43–56.
Ellger, Hans. "Hamburg Neugraben." In *Encyclopedia of Camps and Ghettos, 1933–1945, Vol. 1, B: Early Camps, Youth Camps, and Concentration Camps and Subcamps under the SS-Business Administration Main Office (WVHA)*, edited by Geoffrey Megargee, Rüdiger Overmans, and Wolfgang Vogt, 1122–4. Bloomington: Indiana University Press, 2009. https://doi.org/10.1353/document.2075.
Elman, Amy. "Lesbians and the Holocaust." In *Women and the Holocaust: Narrative and Representation*, edited by Esther Fuchs, 9–19. Lanham, MD: University Press of America, 1999.
Eng, David L. *The Feeling of Kinship: Queer Liberalism and the Racialization of Intimacy*. Durham, NC: Duke University Press, 2010. https://doi.org/10.1515/9780822392828.
Erpel, Simone, ed. *Im Gefolge der SS: Aufseherinnen des Frauen-KZ Ravensbrück*. Berlin: Metropol, 2007.
Eschebach, Insa. "Geschichte und Gedenken: Homophobie, Devianz und weibliche Homosexualität im Konzentrationslager Ravensbrück." In *Homophobie und Devianz: weibliche und männliche Homosexualität im Nationalsozialismus*, edited by Insa Eschebach, 65–79. Berlin: Metropol, 2012. https://doi.org/10.5771/9783748964025.
- "NS-Prozesse in der sowjetischen Besatzungszone und der DDR: einige Überlegungen zu den Strafverfahrensakten ehemaliger

SS-Aufseherinnen des Frauenkonzentrationslagers Ravensbrück." In *Die Frühen Nachkriegsprozesse*, edited by Kurt Buck, 65–74. Bremen: Edition Temmen, 1997.

Evans, Jennifer. "Introduction: Why Queer German History?" *German History* 34, no. 3 (September 2016): 371–84. https://doi.org/10.1093/gerhis/ghw034.

– "Listening for Queer Kinship in Dangerous Times." In *Transatlantische Emanzipationen: Freundschaftsgabe für James Steakley*, edited by Florian Mildenberger, 297–314. Berlin: Männerschwarm, 2021.

– *The Queer Art of History: Queer Kinship after Fascism*. Durham, NC: Duke University Press, 2023. https://doi.org/10.1353/book.110814.

– "Sound, Listening and the Queer Art of History." *Rethinking History* 22, no. 1 (2018): 25–43. https://doi.org/10.1080/13642529.2017.1422584.

Fall, Susanne. *Terezín, ráj mezi lágry*. Prague: Revolver Revue, 2014.

Fitzpatrick, Sheila. "Signals from Below: Soviet Letters of Denunciation of the 1930s." *The Journal of Modern History* 68, no. 4 (December 1996): 831–66. https://doi.org/10.1086/245396.

Flusser, Jindřich. *Život na úvěr*. Prague: Private Printing, 2010.

Folman, Ari, ed., and David Polonsky, illus. *Anne Frank's Diary: The Graphic Adaptation*. London: Viking, 2018.

Fracapane, Silvia Goldbaum Tarabini. *The Jews of Denmark in the Holocaust: Life and Death in Theresienstadt Ghetto*. Abingdon, UK: Routledge, 2021. https://doi.org/10.4324/9780429202827.

Frank, Anne. *Anne Frank Gesamtausgabe. Tagebücher, Geschichten und Ereignisse aus dem Hinterhaus, Erzählungen, Briefe, Fotos und Dokumente*, edited by Mirjam Pressler. Frankfurt am Main: Fischer, 2013.

– *Anne Frank: The Collected Works*, edited by Anne Frank Fonds. London: Bloomsbury, 2019.

Franklin, Ruth. "Beyond the Betrayal." *New York Review of Books*, 26 May 2022.

– *The Many Lives of Anne Frank*. New Haven, NJ: Yale University Press, 2025. https://doi.org/10.12987/9780300281330.

Freedman, Estelle B. "'The Burning of Letters Continues': Elusive Identities and the Historical Construction of Sexuality." *Journal of Women's History* 9, no. 4 (Winter 1998): 181–200. https://doi.org/10.1353/jowh.2010.0237.

Fricker, Miranda. *Epistemic Injustice: Power and the Ethics of Knowing*. Oxford: Oxford University Press, 2007. https://doi.org/10.1093/acprof:oso/9780198237907.001.0001.

Friedman, Saul S., ed. *The Terezin Diary of Gonda Redlich.* Lexington: University Press of Kentucky, 1992.

Frommer, Benjamin. *National Cleansing: Retribution against Nazi Collaborators in Postwar Czechoslovakia.* Cambridge: Cambridge University Press, 2005.

Garbarini, Alexandra. "Document Volumes and the Status of Victim Testimony in the Era of the First World War and Its Aftermath." *Études arméniennes contemporaines* 5 (2015): 113–38. https://doi.org/10.4000/eac.782.

Gelbin, Cathy S. "Double Visions: Queer Femininity and Holocaust Film from *Ostatni Etap* to *Aimée & Jaguar.*" *Women in German Yearbook: Feminist Studies in German Literature & Culture* 23 (2007): 179–204. https://doi.org/10.1353/wgy.2008.0012.

Gerber, Yonah Bex. "As a Queer Jew, Learning Anne Frank Was Bisexual Is a Gamechanger." *Haaretz*, 14 June 2019. https://www.haaretz.com/us-news/2019-06-14/ty-article/as-a-queer-jew-learning-anne-frank-was-bisexual-is-a-game-changer/0000017f-e495-d568-ad7f-f7ffd50a0000.

Giles, Geoffrey J. "Legislating Homophobia in the Third Reich: The Radicalization of Prosecution against Homosexuality by the Legal Profession." *German History* 23, no. 3 (July 2005): 339–54. https://doi.org/10.1191/0266355405gh344oa.

Gleason, Mona. "Avoiding the Agency Trap: Caveats for Historians of Children, Youth, and Education." *History of Education* 45, no. 4 (2016): 446–59. https://doi.org/10.1080/0046760X.2016.1177121.

Glowacka, Dorota. "Sexual Violence against Men and Boys during the Holocaust: A Genealogy of (Not-So-Silent) Silence." *German History* 39, no. 1 (March 2021): 78–99. https://doi.org/10.1093/gerhis/ghaa032.

Goldenberg, Myrna, and Amy Shapiro, eds. *Different Horrors, Same Hell: Gender and the Holocaust.* Seattle: University of Washington Press, 2013. https://doi.org/10.1515/9780295804576.

Grabowski, Jan. Introduction to *Buried Words* by Molly Applebaum, xv–xxxi.

Grau, Günter, ed. *Homosexualität in der NS-Zeit: Dokumente einer Diskriminierung und Verfolgung.* Frankfurt am Main: Fischer Taschenbuch, 2004.

Green, Penelope. "Margot Heuman, Who Bore Witness to the Holocaust as a Gay Woman, Dies at 94." *New York Times*, 27 May 2022. https://

www.nytimes.com/2022/05/27/world/europe/margot-heuman-dead.html.
Greenspan, Henry. "The Unsaid, the Incommunicable, the Unbearable, and the Irretrievable." *The Oral History Review* 41, no. 2 (Summer/Fall 2014): 229–43. https://www.jstor.org/stable/43863584.
Gutterman, Lauren. *Her Neighbor's Wife: A History of Lesbian Desire within Marriage.* Philadelphia: University of Pennsylvania Press, 2019.
Hájková, Anna. "Aus Prag nach San Francisco: die einzigartige Geschichte der lesbischen Widerstandskämpferin Irene Miller." In Arend and Fank, *Ravensbrück denken*, 82–91.
— "Between Love and Coercion: Queer Desire, Sexual Barter and the Holocaust." *German History* 39, no. 1 (March 2021): 112–33. https://doi.org/10.1093/gerhis/ghaa047.
— "Die fabelhaften Jungs aus Theresienstadt: Junge tschechische Männer als dominante soziale Elite im Theresienstädter Ghetto." In *Im Ghetto 1939–1945: neue Forschungen zu Alltag und Umfeld*, edited by Christoph Dieckmann and Babette Quinkert, 116–35. Göttingen: Wallstein, 2009.
— "Har du information om Hambo?" *Berlingske* 2, no. 107, 6 October 2018.
— "Den Holocaust queer erzählen," *Jahrbuch Sexualitäten* 3 (2018): 86–110. https://doi.org/10.5771/9783835343078-86.
— "Introduction: Sexuality, Holocaust, Stigma." *German History* 39, no. 1 (March 2021): 1–14. https://doi.org/10.1093/gerhis/ghaa033.
— *The Last Ghetto: An Everyday History of Theresienstadt.* New York: Oxford University Press, 2020. https://doi.org/10.1093/oso/9780190051778.001.0001.
— "Sexual Barter in Times of Genocide: Negotiating the Sexual Economy of the Theresienstadt Ghetto." *Signs: Journal of Women in Culture and Society* 38, no. 3 (Spring 2013): 503–33. https://doi.org/10.1086/668607.
— "Why We Need a History of Prostitution in the Holocaust." *European Review of History/Revue européenne d'histoire* 29, no. 2 (2022): 194–222. https://doi.org/10.1080/13507486.2022.2028739.
Hájková, Anna, Karolina Krasuska, Max Strassfeld, Gregg Drinkwater, Aleksandra Gajowy, Mir Yarfitz, Rafael Balling, and Carli Snyder. "Queering Jewish Studies." *Jewish Social Studies* 29, no. 2 (Spring/Summer 2024): 1–33. https://doi.org/10.2979/jss.00007.
Halbmayr, Brigitte. *Zeitlebens konsequent: Hermann Langbein, 1912–1995; eine politische Biografie.* Vienna: Braumüller, 2012.

Hallama, Peter. "'A Great Civic and Scientific Duty of Our Historiography': Czech Historians and the Holocaust in the 1970s and 1980s." In *Growing in the Shadow of Antifascism: Remembering the Holocaust in State-Socialist Eastern Europe*, edited by Kata Bohus, Peter Hallama, and Stephan Stach, 39–62. Budapest: Central European University Press, 2022. https://doi.org/10.7829/j.ctv280b7j3.

Hann, Cheryl D. "'If only I had a girlfriend!': Towards a Queer Reading of *The Diary of a Young Girl*." Master's thesis, Dalhousie University, 2016.

Harris, Elizabeth A., and Alexandra Alter. "With Rising Book Bans, Librarians Have Come Under Attack." *New York Times*, 6 July 2022. https://www.nytimes.com/2022/07/06/books/book-ban-librarians.html.

Hart, Lynda. *Fatal Women: Lesbian Sexuality and the Mark of Aggression*. London: Routledge, 1994. https://doi.org/10.1515/9780691261188.

Healey, Dan. *Russian Homophobia from Stalin to Sochi*. London: Bloomsbury, 2018.

Heger, Heinz. *The Men with the Pink Triangle*. Translated by David Fernbach. London: GMP, 1980.

Heineman, Elizabeth D. "Sexuality and Nazism: The Doubly Unspeakable?" *Journal of the History of Sexuality* 11, nos. 1/2 (January–April 2002): 22–66. https://www.jstor.org/stable/3704551.

Helm, Sarah. *If This Is a Woman: Inside Ravensbruck: Hitler's Concentration Camp for Women*. London: Abacus, 2015.

Herrn, Rainer. "Transvestitismus in der NS-Zeit: Ein Forschungsdesiderat." *Zeitschrift für Sexualforschung* 26, no. 4 (2013): 330–71. https://doi.org/10.1055/s-0033-1356172.

Herzog, Dagmar. *Sexuality in Europe: A Twentieth-Century History*. Cambridge: Cambridge University Press, 2011. https://doi.org/10.1017/CBO9780511997075.

"A Holocaust Survivor's Frank Story." *Washington Times*, 7 August 2004. https://www.washingtontimes.com/news/2004/aug/7/20040807-112350-1209r/.

Horowitz, Sara R. "'If He Knows to Make a Child ... ': Memories of Birth and Baby-Killing in Deferred Jewish Testimony Narratives." In *Jewish Histories of the Holocaust: New Transnational Approaches*, edited by Norman J.W. Goda, 135–51. New York: Berghahn, 2014. https://doi.org/10.1515/9781782384427-009.

– "What We Learn, at Last: Recounting Sexuality in Women's Deferred Autobiographies and Testimonies." In *The Palgrave Handbook of Holocaust Literature and Culture*, edited by Victoria Aarons and Phyllis Lassner, 45–66. Cham: Palgrave Macmillan, 2020. https://doi.org/10.1007/978-3-030-33428-4.

Janz, Ulrike. "Das Zeichen lesbisch in den nationalsozialistischen Konzentrationslagern." In *Homosexuelle im Nationalsozialismus: Neue Forschungsperspektiven zu Lebenssituationen von lesbischen, schwulen, bi-, trans- und intersexuellen Menschen 1933 bis 1945*, edited by Michael Schwartz, 77–84. Munich: De Gruyter Oldenbourg, 2014. https://doi.org/10.1524/9783486857504.

– "Zeugnisse überlebender Frauen. Die Wahrnehmung von Lesben/Lesbischem Verhalten in nationalsozialistischen Konzentrationslagern." *Frauenzeitung*, no. 2 (1994): 21–25, 48–50; no. 3 (1994): 20–23, 40–41; no. 1 (1995): 48–51.

Jockusch, Laura. *Collect and Record! Jewish Holocaust Documentation in Early Postwar Europe*. Oxford: Oxford University Press, 2012. https://doi.org/10.1093/acprof:oso/9780199764556.001.0001.

Johansson, Warren, and William A. Percy. "Homosexuals in Nazi Germany." *Simon Wiesenthal Center* 7 (1990): ch. 12, part 1.

Jones, William Ross. "'You Are Going to Be My *Bettmann*': Exploitative Sexual Relationships and the Lives of the *Pipels* in Nazi Concentration Camps." *The Journal of Holocaust Research* 38, nos. 3–4 (2024): 253–72. https://doi.org/10.1080/25785648.2024.2363682.

Joscowicz, Ari. *Rain of Ash: Roma, Jews, and the Holocaust*. Princeton, NJ: Princeton University Press, 2023. https://doi.org/10.1353/book.110826.

Jureit, Ulrike. *Erinnerungsmuster: zur Methodik lebensgeschichtlicher Interviews mit Überlebenden der Konzentrations- und Vernichtungslager*. Hamburg: Ergebnisse, 1999.

Kämper, Dirk. *Fredy Hirsch und die Kinder des Holocaust*. Zurich: Orrel Füssli, 2015.

Karczewski, Kamil. "Transnational Flows of Knowledge and the Legalisation of Homosexuality in Interwar Poland." *Contemporary European History* 33, no. 3 (August 2024): 849–66. https://doi.org/10.1017/S0960777322000108.

Kárný, Miroslav. "Fragen zum 8. März 1944." In *Theresienstädter Studien und Dokumente: 1999*, edited by Jaroslava Milotová, 9–42. Prague: Sefer, 1999.

– "Terezínský rodinný tábor v 'Konečném řešení.'" In *Terezínský rodinný tábor v Osvětimi-Birkenau*, edited by Toman Brod, Miroslav Kárný, and Margita Kárná, 35–49. Prague: Melantrich, 1994.

Kassow, Samuel D. *Who Will Write Our History? Emanuel Ringelblum, the Warsaw Ghetto, and the Oyneg Shabes Archive*. Bloomington: Indiana University Press, 2007.

Knoll, Albert. "'Es muss alles versucht werden, um dieses widernatürliche Laster auszurotten': Homosexuelle Häftlinge in den frühen Konzentrationslagern." In " … *der schrankenlosesten Willkür ausgeliefert": Häftlinge der frühen Konzentrationslager 1933–1936/37*, edited by Jörg Osterloh and Kim Wünschmann, 221–45. Frankfurt am Main: Campus, 2017.

Kogon, Eugen. *Der SS-Staat*. Stockholm: Bermann-Fischer, 1947.

Korbel, Susanne. "Portrayals of a Female Impersonator: Visual Representations of Gender-Bending between Central Europe and the United States." *Zeitgeschichte* 50, no. 1 (April 2023): 93–114. https://doi.org/10.14220/zsch.2023.50.1.93.

Kosta, Jiří. *Život mezi úzkostí a nadějí*. Prague: Paseka, 2002.

Kraus, Ota, and Erich Kulka. *Death Factory: Document on Auschwitz*. Oxford: Pergamon, 1966.

Kretzer, Anette. *NS-Täterschaft und Geschlecht: der erste britische Ravensbrück-Prozess 1946/47 in Hamburg*. Berlin: Metropol, 2009.

Kuntsman, Adi. "Between Gulags and Pride Parades: Sexuality, Nation, and Haunted Speech Acts." *GLQ* 14, nos. 2–3 (2008): 263–87. https://muse.jhu.edu/article/241328.

Kunzel, Regina G. *Criminal Intimacy: Prison and the Uneven History of Modern American Sexuality*. Chicago: University of Chicago Press, 2002.

– "The Power of Queer History." *The American Historical Review* 123, no. 5 (December 2018): 1560–82. https://www.jstor.org/stable/26581553.

– "Situating Sex: Prison Sexual Culture in the Mid-Twentieth-Century United States." *GLQ: A Journal of Lesbian and Gay Studies* 8, no. 3 (2002): 253–70. https://muse.jhu.edu/article/12212.

Kurimay, Anita. *Queer Budapest, 1873–1961*. Chicago: University of Chicago Press, 2020. https://doi.org/10.7208/chicago/9780226705828.001.0001.

Kwiet, Konrad, and Helmut Eschwege. *Selbstbehauptung und Widerstand: deutsche Juden im Kampf um Existenz und Menschenwürde, 1933–1945*. Hamburg: Christians, 1984.

LaFleur, Greta, Masha Raskolnikov, and Anna Kłosowska, eds. *Trans Historical: Gender Plurality before the Modern*. Ithaca, NY: Cornell University Press, 2021. https://doi.org/10.7591/cornell/9781501759086.001.0001.

Langbein, Hermann. *People in Auschwitz*. Translated by Harry Zohn. Chapel Hill: University of North Carolina Press, 2006.

Langer, Lawrence L. *Admitting the Holocaust: Collected Essays*. New York: Oxford University Press, 1995. https://doi.org/10.1093/oso/9780195093575.001.0001.

– "Remembering Survival," in *Holocaust Remembrance: The Shapes of Memory*, edited by Geoffrey Hartman, 70–80. Oxford: Oxford University Press, 1994.

Lapin, Andrew. "Anne Frank's Diary, 'Schindler's List' among Titles at Center of Major Florida Book-Ban Lawsuit." *Jewish Telegraphic Agency*, 10 January 2024. https://www.jta.org/2024/01/10/united-states/anne-franks-diary-schindlers-list-among-titles-at-center-of-major-florida-book-ban-lawsuit.

– "Meet Bruce Friedman, the Jewish Dad Who Got a Version of Anne Frank's Diary and Hundreds of Other Books Banned from His Florida School District." *Jewish Telegraphic Agency*, 6 October 2023. https://www.jta.org/2023/10/06/united-states/this-jewish-dad-got-a-version-of-anne-franks-diary-removed-from-his-florida-school-district.

Laub, Dori. "Breaking the Silence of the Muted Witnesses: Video Testimonies of the Psychiatrically Hospitalized Holocaust Survivors in Israel." *Lessons and Legacies, Vol. 8: From Generation to Generation*, edited by Doris Bergen, 175–90. Evanston: Northwestern University Press, 2008. https://doi.org/10.2307/j.ctv47w6md.

Lebovic, Matt. "Who Was Anne Frank's Gay Uncle Walter?" *Times of Israel*, 23 May 2018. https://www.timesofisrael.com/who-was-anne-franks-gay-uncle-walter/.

Leff, Lisa. *The Archive Thief: The Man Who Salvaged French Jewish History in the Wake of the Holocaust*. Oxford: Oxford University Press, 2015.

Leipciger, Nathan. *The Weight of Freedom*, 3rd ed. Toronto: Azrieli Foundation, 2019.

Ley, Astrid. "Sexualität im Männer-KZ zwischen Gewalterfahrung und Tauschverhältnis: Zum Schicksal des Pogrom-Häftlings Siegfried H. im KZ Sachsenhausen." In Arend and Fank, *Ravensbrück denken*, 52–60.

Lochrie, Karma. "Have We Ever Been Normal?" In *Heterosyncrasies. Female Sexuality When Normal Wasn't*, edited by Karma Lochrie, 1–25. Minneapolis: University of Minnesota Press, 2005.

Lower, Wendy. *The Ravine: A Family, a Photograph, a Holocaust Massacre Revealed*. New York: Harper Collins, 2021.

Lustig, Arnošt. *Night and Hope*. Translated by George Theiner. Iowa City: University of Iowa Press, 1973.

Lybeck, Marti M. *Desiring Emancipation: New Women and Homosexuality in Germany, 1890–1933*. Albany: State University of New York Press, 2014. https://doi.org/10.1353/book34065.

Macadam, Heather Dune. *999: The Extraordinary Young Women of the First Official Jewish Transport to Auschwitz*. New York: Citadel, 2019.

Mailänder, Elissa. "Meshes of Power: The Concentration Camp as Pulp or Art House in Liliana Cavani's 'The Night Porter.'" In *Nazisploitation! The Nazi Image in Low-Brow Cinema and Culture*, edited by Daniel H. Magilow, Elizabeth Bridges, and Kristin T. Vander Lugt, 175–95. London: Bloomsbury, 2012. https://doi.org/10.5040/9781628928228.

Makarova, Elena. *Closer to the Truth: Terezín Cartoonist Erich Lichtblau-Leský*. Lochamei Haghettaot: Lochamei Haghettaot Press, 2011.

Marhoefer, Laurie. "Lesbianism, Transvestitism, and the Nazi State: A Microhistory of a Gestapo Investigation, 1939–1943." *The American Historical Review* 121, no. 4 (October 2016): 1167–95. https://doi.org/10.1093/ahr/121.4.1167.

– *Racism and the Making of Gay Rights: A Sexologist, His Student, and the Empire of Queer Love*. Toronto: University of Toronto Press, 2022. https://doi.org/10.3138/9781487532741.

– *Sex and the Weimar Republic: German Homosexual Emancipation and the Rise of the Nazis*. Toronto: University of Toronto Press, 2015.

– "Transgender Life and Persecution under the Nazi State: *Gutachten* on the Vollbrecht Case." *Central European History* 56, no. 4 (December 2023): 595–601. https://doi.org/10.1017/S0008938923000468.

Maynes, Mary Jo. "Age as a Category of Historical Analysis: History, Agency, and Narratives of Childhood." *The Journal of the History of Childhood and Youth* 1, no. 1 (Winter 2008): 114–24. https://doi.org/10.1353/hcy.2008.0001.

McGrane, Sally. "A Fight Over Anne Frank's Fallen Tree." *New York Times*, 8 June 2011. https://www.nytimes.com/2011/06/09/world/europe/09tree.html.

Melamed, Vladimir, ed. *They Shall Be Counted: The Theresienstadt Ghetto Art of Erich Lichtblau-Leskly*. Los Angeles: Los Angelos Museum of the Holocaust, 2010.

Meyer, Beate. *A Fatal Balancing Act: The Dilemma of the Reich Association of Jews in Germany, 1939–1945*. Translated by William Templer. New York: Berghahn, 2016.

Mikel Arieli, Roni. "Reading *The Diary of Anne Frank* on Robben Island: On the Role of Holocaust Memory in Ahmed Kathrada's Struggle against Apartheid." *Journal of Jewish Identities* 12, no. 2 (July 2019): 175–95. https://doi.org/10.1353/jji.2019.0018.

Mikovcová, Alena. "Brněnské období Fredyho Hirsche." *Židé a Morava* 18 (2011): 124–40.

Milton, Sybil. "Women and the Holocaust: The Case of German and German-Jewish Women." In *When Biology Became Destiny: Women in Weimar and Nazi Germany*, edited by Renate Bridenthal, Atina Grossmann, and Marion A. Kaplan, 297–333. New York: Monthly Review Press, 1984.

Mühlhäuser, Regina. *Eroberungen: sexuelle Gewalttaten und intime Beziehungen deutscher Soldaten in der Sowjetunion 1941–1945*. Hamburg: Hamburger Edition, 2010.

Müller, Joachim, and Andreas Sternweiler, eds. *Homosexuelle Männer im KZ Sachsenhausen*. Berlin: Rosa Winkel, 2000.

Müller, Melissa. *Anne Frank: The Biography*. London: Bloomsbury, 2013.

Nestle, Joan. "Review: Into the Mainstream." *Bridges* 1, no. 1 (Spring 1990/5750): 98–104. https://www.jstor.org/stable/40357413.

Newsome, W. Jake. *Pink Triangle Legacies: Coming Out in the Shadow of the Holocaust*. Ithaca: Cornell University Press, 2022. https://doi.org/10.7591/cornell/9781501765155.001.0001.

Nunn, Zavier. "Trans Liminality and the Nazi State." *Past & Present* 260, no. 1 (August 2023): 123–57. https://doi.org/10.1093/pastj/gtac018.

Ondřichová, Lucie. *Příběh Fredyho Hirsche*. Prague: Sefer, 2001.

Oppenhejm, Ralph. *An der Grenze des Lebens: Theresienstädter Tagebuch*. Hamburg: Rueten & Loening, 1961.

Ostrowska, Joanna. *Jene: Homosexuelle während des Zweiten Weltkriegs*. Translated by Beate Kosmala. Berlin: Metropol, 2023.

— "'Solche Berichte interessierten mich nie': lesbische Frauen in Erinnerungen ehemaliger weiblicher Häftlinge des KZ Auschwitz." In Ostrowska, Talewicz-Kwiatkowska, and van Dijk, *Erinnern in Auschwitz*, 83–100.

Ostrowska, Joanna, Joanna Talewicz-Kwiatkowska, and Lutz van Dijk, eds. *Erinnern in Auschwitz: auch an sexuelle Minderheiten*. Berlin: Querverlag, 2020.

Ostrowska, Joanna, and Lutz van Dijk. "'Pipels und Puppenjungen': über sexuellen Missbrauch an Jungen und Männern in Auschwitz." In Ostrowska, Talewicz-Kwiatkowska, and van Dijk, *Erinnern in Auschwitz*, 113–26.

Overing, Joanna, Paolo Fortis, and Margherita Margiotti. "Kinship in Anthropology." In *International Encyclopedia of the Social & Behavioral Sciences*, edited by James D. Wright, 36–43. Amsterdam: Elsevier, 2015. https://doi.org/10.1016/B978-0-08-097086-8.12098-7.

Pająk, Paulina. "'Echo Texts': Woolf, Krzywicka, and *The Well of Loneliness*." *Woolf Studies Annual* 24 (2018): 11–34.

Pawełczynska, Anna. *Values and Violence in Auschwitz: A Sociological Analysis*. Berkeley: University of California Press, 1979.

Penn, Donna. "Queer: Theorizing Politics and History." *Radical History Review* 62 (Spring 1995): 24–42. https://doi.org/10.1215/01636545-1995-62-24.

Piper, Franciszek. "Blechhammer." In *Encyclopedia of Camps and Ghettos, 1933–1945, Vol. 1, A: The Early National Socialist Concentration Camps*, edited by Geoffrey P. Megargee, 227–8. Bloomington: Indiana University Press, 2009. https://doi.org/10.1353/document.1381.

Pollak, Michael. *Die Grenzen des Sagbaren: Lebensgeschichten von KZ-Überlebenden als Augenzeugenberichte und als Identitätsarbeit*. Frankfurt am Main: Campus Verlag, 1988.

Pollin-Gallay, Hannah. *Occupied Words: What the Holocaust Did to Yiddish*. Philadelphia: University of Pennsylvania Press, 2024. https://doi.org/10.2307/jj.6605413.

Portmann, John. *Women and Gay Men in the Postwar Period*. London: Bloomsbury Academic, 2016.

Rachamimov, Iris. "From Lesbian Radicalism to Trans-Masculine Innovation: The Queer Place of Jerusalem in Israeli LGBT Geographies (1979–2007)." *Geography Research Forum* 39, no. 1 (2019): 19–42.

Rautenberg, Uta. *Homophobia in Nazi Camps*. Toronto: University of Toronto Press, forthcoming.

Rautenberg, Viola. "Homosexuality, Resistance and Aftermath: Gad Beck, Jizchak Schwersenz, and the 'Chug Chaluzi' in Berlin Underground 1943–1945." Paper presented at the conference Queer

Experiences during the Third Reich and the Holocaust, University of Haifa, 7 May 2009.

— *Zwischen Ideologie und Überleben. Der Chug Chaluzi im Berliner Untergrund 1943–1945*. Master's thesis, Hamburg University, 2008.

— "Zwischen Ideologie und Überleben: Offene Fragen zum 'Chug Chaluzi' im Berliner Untergrund 1943–1945." *Transversal: Zeitschrift für jüdische Studien* 2 (2010): 51–71.

Redlich, Egon. *Zítra jedeme, synu, pojedeme transportem: deník Egona Redlicha z Terezína 1.1.1942–22.10.1944*, edited by Miroslav Kryl. Brno: Doplněk, 1995.

Rheinberg, Bernd, and Susanne Dittrich. *Jahresbericht 2000*. Heinrich Böll Stiftung e.V., 2000. https://www.boell.de/sites/default/files/jb2000.pdf.

Rich, Adrienne. "Compulsory Heterosexuality and Lesbian Existence." *Signs* 5, no. 4 (Summer 1980): 631–60. https://doi.org/10.1086/493756.

Rieder, Ines. *Heimliches Begehren: die Geschichte der Sidonie C.* Vienna: Deuticke, 2000.

Robinson, Paul. "Opera Queen: A Voice from the Closet." *Cambridge Opera Journal* 6, no. 3 (November 1994): 283–91. https://doi.org/10.1017/S095458670000433X.

Röll, Wolfgang. "Homosexual Inmates in the Buchenwald Concentration Camp." *Journal of Homosexuality* 31, no. 4 (1996): 1–28. https://doi.org/10.1300/J082v31n04_01.

Rose, Julia. *Interpreting Difficult History at Museums and Historic Sites*. Lanham, MD: Rowman & Littlefield, 2016. https://doi.org/10.5771/9780759124387.

Rousset, David. *A World Apart*. London: Secker and Wartburg, 1951.

Rubin, Eli. "Epilogue: Doing Straight Time in Honecker's GDR." In *Socialist Subjectivities: Rethinking East Germany*, edited by Jeff Hayton, Katherine White, and Scot Harrison, 290–306. Ann Arbor: University of Michigan Press, 2025.

Samper Vendrell, Javier. "The Case of a German-Jewish Lesbian Woman: Martha Mosse and the Danger of Standing Out." *German Studies Review* 41, no. 2 (May 2018): 335–53. https://doi.org/10.1353/gsr.2018.0058.

— *The Seduction of Youth: Print Culture and Homosexual Rights in the Weimar Republic*. Toronto: University of Toronto Press, 2020. https://doi.org/10.3138/9781487536053.

Sawicka, Barbara. "Fünfteichen." In *Encyclopedia of Camps and Ghettos, 1933–1945, Vol. 1, B: Early Camps, Youth Camps, and Concentration Camps and Subcamps under the SS-Business Administration Main Office (WVHA)*, edited by Geoffrey Megargee, Rüdiger Overmans, and Wolfgang Vogt, 729–31. Bloomington: Indiana University Press, 2009. https://doi.org/10.1353/document.1767.

— "Fünfteichen (Miłoszyce koło Wrocławia)." In *Der Ort des Terrors: Geschichte der nationalsozialistischen Konzentrationslager, Vol. 6: Natzweiler, Groß-Rosen, Stutthof*, edited by Wolfgang Benz and Barbara Distel, 295–301. Munich: Beck, 2007.

Schoppmann, Claudia. "'Liebe wurde mit Prügelstrafe geahndet': zur Situation lesbischer Frauen in den Konzentrationslagern." *Verfolgung von Homosexuellen im Nationalsozialismus* 5 (1999): 14–21.

— *Nationalsozialistische Sexualpolitik und weibliche Homosexualität*, 2nd ed. Herbolzheim: Centaurus, 1997. https://doi.org/10.1007/978-3-86226-853-5.

— *Zeit der Maskierung: Lebensgeschichten lesbischer Frauen im Dritten Reich*. Berlin: Orlanda Frauenverlag, 1993.

Schraub, David. "White Jews: An Intersectional Approach." *AJS Review: The Journal of the Association for Jewish Studies* 43, no. 2 (November 2019): 379–407. https://doi.org/10.1017/s0364009419000461.

Schüler-Springorum, Stefanie. "Homophobe Erinnerungen: eine Analyse von Zeitzeugnissen des Holocaust." In Arend and Fank, *Ravensbrück denken*, 74–81.

Schwersenz, Jizchak. *Die versteckte Gruppe: ein jüdischer Lehrer erinnert sich an Deutschland*. Berlin: Wichern-Verlag, 1988.

Seidl, Jan, Jan Wintr, and Lukáš Nozar. *Od žaláře k oltáři: emancipace homosexuality v českých zemích od roku 1867 do současnosti*. Brno: Host, 2012.

Serotta, Edward. *Out of the Shadows: A Photographic Portrait of Jewish Life in Central Europe since the Holocaust*. Secaucus, NJ: Carol Pub. Group, 1991.

Shenker, Noah. *Reframing Holocaust Testimony*. Bloomington: Indiana University Press, 2015.

Siegel, Sari J. "Treating an Auschwitz Prisoner-Physician: The Case of Dr. Maximilian Samuel." *Holocaust and Genocide Studies* 28, no. 3 (Winter 2014): 450–81. https://doi.org/10.1093/hgs/dcu041.

Sienna, Noam, ed. *A Rainbow Thread: An Anthology of Queer Jewish Texts from the First Century to 1969*. Philadelphia: Print-O-Craft, 2019.

Sköld, Johanna, and Ingrid Söderlind. "Agentic Subjects and Objects of Political Propaganda: Swedish Media Representations of Children in the Mobilization for Supporting Finland During World War II." *The Journal of the History of Childhood and Youth* 11, no. 1 (Winter 2018): 27–46. https://doi.org/10.1353/hcy.2018.0002.

Sliwa, Joanna. *Jewish Childhood in Kraków: A Microhistory of the Holocaust.* New Brunswick, NJ: Rutgers University Press, 2021. https://doi.org/10.36019/9781978822979.

Smith-Rosenberg, Carroll. "The Female World of Love and Ritual: Relations between Women in Nineteenth-Century America." *Signs* 1, no. 1 (Autumn 1975): 1–29. https://www.jstor.org/stable/3172964.

Sommer, Robert. *Das KZ-Bordell: sexuelle Zwangsarbeit in nationalsozialistischen Konzentrationslagern.* Paderborn: Schöningh, 2009. https://doi.org/10.30965/9783657765249.

– "Pipels: Situational Homosexual Slavery of Young Adolescent Boys in Nazi Concentration Camps." In *Lessons and Legacies, Vol. 11: Expanding Perspectives on the Holocaust in a Changing World*, edited by Hilary Earl and Karl A. Schleunes, 86–103. Evanston, Illinois: Northwestern University Press, 2014. https://doi.org/10.2307/j.ctv47wb5x.

Spivak, Gayatri Chakravorty. "Can the Subaltern Speak?" In *Marxism and the Interpretation of Culture*, edited by Cary Nelson and Lawrence Grossberg, 271–313. Urbana: University of Illinois Press, 1988.

Spurlin, William J. *Lost Intimacies: Rethinking Homosexuality under National Socialism.* New York: Peter Lang, 2009. https://doi.org/10.3726/978-1-4539-0138-0.

Stengel, Katharina. *Hermann Langbein: ein Auschwitz-Überlebender in den erinnerungspolitischen Konflikten der Nachkriegszeit.* Frankfurt: Campus, 2012.

Stephens, Elizabeth. "'Unhallowed Arts': Or, the Science of Making Monsters." In *Unhallowed Arts*, edited by Laetitia Wilson, Oron Catts, and Eugenio Viola, 119–127. Perth: University of Western Australia, 2018.

Strassfeld, Max K. *Trans Talmud: Androgynes and Eunuchs in Rabbinic Literature.* Berkeley: University of California Press, 2022. https://doi.org/10.1525/9780520382060.

Stryker, Susan. *Transgender History.* Berkeley: Seal Press, 2008.

Suderland, Maja. *Inside Concentration Camps: Social Life at the Extremes.* Translated by Jessica Spengler. Cambridge: Polity, 2013.

Sullivan, Rosemary. *The Betrayal of Anne Frank: A Cold Case Investigation.* New York: Harper Perennial, 2022.

Sutton, Katie. *Sexuality in Modern German History.* London: Bloomsbury, 2023. https://doi.org/10.5040/9781350010109.

Švalbová, Manca. *Vyhasnuté oči: Requiem.* Bratislava: Nakladateľstvo Pravda, 1949.

Tesař, Jan. "Miroslav Kárný. Studie o vlivu ideologie a politické moci na jedince v letech 1919–1974." BA thesis, Charles University, 2010.

Timm, Annette F. "The Challenges of Including Sexual Violence and Transgressive Love in Historical Writing on World War II and the Holocaust." *Journal of the History of Sexuality* 26, no. 3 (September 2017): 351–65. https://www.jstor.org/stable/44862403.

Tomek, Prokop. "Svazek StB jako historický pramen." *Soudobé dějiny* 12, no. 1 (2005): 208–14.

Tremblay, Sébastien. *A Badge of Injury: The Pink Triangle as Global Symbol of Memory.* Berlin: De Gruyter Oldenbourg, 2024. https://doi.org/10.1515/9783111067711.

– "'Ich konnte ihren Schmerz körperlich spüren': die Historisierung der NS-Verfolgung und die Wiederaneignung des Rosa Winkels in der westdeutschen Schwulenbewegung der 1970er Jahre." *Invertito*, no. 21 (2019), 179–202.

Van der Boom, Bart, and Laurien Vastenhout. "Réfutation du livre *The Betrayal of Anne Frank (Qui a Trahi Anne Frank?)* de Rosemary Sullivan." *Revue d'Histoire de la Shoah* 216, no. 2 (2022): 335–58. https://doi.org/10.3917/rhsho.216.0335.

Van Dijk, Lutz. *"Ein erfülltes Leben – trotzdem ... " Erinnerungen Homosexueller 1933–1945.* Reinbek bei Hamburg: Rowohlt, 1992.

–, ed. *Einsam war ich nie: Schwule unter dem Hakenkreuz 1933–1945.* Berlin: Querverlag, 2003.

– "In Auschwitz hatte ich meine größte Liebe ... " In Van Dijk, *Einsam war ich nie*, 54–63.

Van Liempt, Ilse. "Trafficking in Human Beings: Conceptual Dilemmas." In *Trafficking and Women's Rights*, edited by Christien van den Anker and Jeroen Doomernik, 27–42. New York: Palgrave, 2006.

Van Maarsen, Jacqueline. *My Name Is Anne, She Said, Anne Frank.* London: Arcadia, 2007.

Volkov, Shulamit. "Antisemitism as a Cultural Code: Reflections on the History and Historiography of Antisemitism in Imperial Germany."

Leo Baeck Institute Yearbook 23, no. 1 (January 1978): 25–46. https://doi.org/10.1093/leobaeck/23.1.25.

Von der Heydt, Maria. "'Wer fährt denn gerne mit dem Judenstern in der Straßenbahn?' Die Ambivalenz des 'geltungsjüdischen' Alltags zwischen 1941 und 1945." In *Alltag im Holocaust: Jüdisches Leben im Großdeutschen Reich 1941–1945*, edited by Doris L. Bergen, Andrea Löw, and Anna Hájková, 65–80. Munich: Oldenbourg, 2013. https://doi.org/10.1524/9783486735673.65.

Wachsmann, Nikolaus. *KL: A History of the Nazi Concentration Camps*. London: Farrar, Straus and Giroux, 2015.

Walke, Anika. *Pioneers and Partisans: An Oral History of Nazi Genocide in Belorussia*. New York: Oxford University Press, 2015. https://doi.org/10.1093/acprof:oso/9780199335534.001.0001.

—. "Review of *The Ravine: A Family, a Photograph, a Holocaust Massacre Revealed*, by Wendy Lower." *AJS Review: The Journal of the Association for Jewish Studies* 47, no. 1 (April 2023): 238–40. https://doi.org/10.1353/ajs.2023.0035.

Walters, Tracey L. "Overview: The History of Black Women's Domestic Labor from the Twentieth Century to the Present." In *Not Your Mother's Mammy: The Black Domestic Worker in Transatlantic Women's Media*, 13–26. New Brunswick, NJ: Rutgers University Press, 2021. https://doi.org/10.36019/9781978808614.

Waxman, Zoë. *Women and the Holocaust: A Feminist History*. Oxford: Oxford University Press, 2017. https://doi.org/10.1093/acprof:oso/9780199608683.001.0001.

Weston, Kath. *Families We Choose: Lesbians, Gays, Kinship*. New York: Columbia University Press, 1991.

Williams, Kieran, and Dennis Deletant. *Security Intelligence Services in New Democracies: The Czech Republic, Slovakia and Romania*. Basingstoke, UK: Palgrave Macmillan, 2001. https://doi.org/10.1057/9781403905369.

Wolfert, Raimund. *Charlotte Charlaque: Transfrau, Laienschauspielerin, "Königin" der Brooklyn Heights Promenade*. Leipzig: Hentrich & Hentrich, 2021.

Wünschmann, Kim, *Before Auschwitz: Jewish Prisoners in the Prewar Concentration Camps*. Cambridge, MA: Harvard University Press, 2015. https://doi.org/10.4159/9780674425569.

—, ed. *"Das Glück kam immer zu mir": Rudolf Brazda, das Überleben eines Homosexuellen im Dritten Reich*. Frankfurt am Main: Campus, 2011.

Zabransky, Florian. "Male Jewish Teenage Sexuality in Nazi Germany." In *If This Is a Woman: Studies on Women and Gender in the Holocaust*, edited by Denisa Nešťáková, Katja Grosse-Sommer, Borbála Klacsmann, and Jakub Drábik, 243–63. Boston: Academic Studies Press, 2021. https://doi.org/10.1515/9781644697115.

Zinn, Alexander. *"Aus dem Volkskörper entfernt"? Homosexuelle Männer im Nationalsozialismus*. Frankfurt: Campus, 2018.

Online Sources and Films

Bloudek, František. Interview. *Paměť národa*. https://www.pametnaroda.cz/cs/bloudek-frantisek-1947.

Brod, Toman. Interview. *Paměť národa*. https://www.pametnaroda.cz/cs/brod-toman-20140221.

Bourdeau, Noë. "'I Am Jeopardizing Everyone Wherever I Go': Toward a Trans* History of the Holocaust." Lecture, Midwest Center for Holocaust Education, Kansas City, 5 October 2023, 55:47. https://www.youtube.com/watch?v=xKGZEqDgMj8.

Cantillon, Lauren. "Challenging the Shame Paradigm: Jewish Women's Narratives of Sexual(ised) Violence during the Holocaust." Lecture, USC Dornsife Center for Advanced Genocide Research, 25 March 2021, 1:33:15. https://www.youtube.com/watch?v=6TIjl0WUkbY.

Centropa. "Preserving Jewish Memory. Bringing History to Life." www.centropa.org/en.

"CS/CS/HB 1069: Education." The Florida Senate, 1 July 2023. https://www.flsenate.gov/Session/Bill/2023/1069/?Tab=BillHistory.

"Diviš Václav & Divišová Karla." *Yad Vashem*. https://collections.yadvashem.org/en/righteous/4036229.

Does, Carsten, and Robin Cackett, dirs. *Die Freiheit des Erzählens: Das Leben des Gad Beck*. Germany, 2006.

Frank, Anne. *Anne Frank Manuscripten*. https://annefrankmanuscripten.org.

Funke, Jana. "The World and Other Unpublished Works of Radclyffe Hall." *Notches* (blog), 24 July 2018. https://notchesblog.com/2018/07/24/the-world-and-other-unpublished-works-of-radclyffe-hall/.

Gat, Rubi, dir. *Freddy HaYakar*. Israel, 2017.

Hájková, Anna. "Fredy Hirsch's Lover: Could a Homosexual Love Survive Theresienstadt?" *Tablet* (blog), 2 May 2019. https://www.tabletmag.com/sections/arts-letters/articles/fredy-hirschs-lover.

– "Queer Desire in the Holocaust: 'I Did Not Want to Die without Having Kissed a Woman.'" Lecture, USC Shoah Foundation: Recovering Victims' Voices Lecture Series, 29 March 2024, 1:12:42. https://www.youtube.com/watch?v=6ZZGXnYc2Ok.

Heuman, Margot. Interview by Carolyn Richmond. *Surviving Together/Queer Holocaust Survivor Margot Heuman(n)/Pride Month*, USC Shoah Foundation, 2 December 1994, 2:18:57. https://www.youtube.com/watch?v=QYiOCT48xwE&t=1s.

Jackman, Josh. "Anne Frank Was Attracted to Girls." *Pink News*, 7 September 2017. https://www.thepinknews.com/2024/06/12/anne-frank-was-attracted-to-girls/.

Mauthausen Memorial. "Queere Lagergeschichte(n) – Erinnerungen, Diskurse, Kontinuitäten," Workshop at the 14th Dialogforum 2023, KZ-Gedenkstätte Mauthausen, 29–30 September 2023. https://vimeo.com/user129634459.

Müller, Klaus, cur. "Do You Remember, When." United States Holocaust Memorial Museum. https://www.ushmm.org/collections/the-museums-collections/collections-highlights/do-you-remember-when.

Nemerofsky Ramsay, Benny. *The Muranów Lily*. Warsaw: POLIN: Museum of the History of Polish Jews, 2015. https://www.polin.pl/en/benny-nemerofsky-ramsay.

Nestle, Joan. "The Kiss, 1950s–1990s." *Outhistory* (blog), 2011. http://outhistory.org/exhibits/show/historical-musings/the-kiss.

Pavlát, Leo. "Propagátor české židovské kultury Jiří Vrba." *Český rozhlas*, 15 June 2014. https://temata.rozhlas.cz/propagator-ceske-zidovske-kultury-jiri-vrba-7995227.

Potužil, Zdeněk. Interview. *Paměť národa*. https://www.pametnaroda.cz/cs/potuzil-zdenek-20160629-0.

Růžička, Jan, dir. *Queer*. Season 11, episode 8, "Fredy. Hagibor. Hrdina." Czech Republic, 2018.

Shainmain, Jon. "'Anne Frank's Diary: The Graphic Adaptation' Removed from Vero Beach High School Library." *WPTV*, 5 April 2023. https://www.wptv.com/news/education/anne-franks-diary-the-graphic-adaptation-removed-from-vero-beach-high-school-library.

Snyder, Carli. "Questions of Gender and Sexuality in Interviewer Trainings and Holocaust Survivor Testimonies." Lecture, USC Dornsife Center for Advanced Genocide Research, 6 February 2023, 1:37:47. https://www.youtube.com/watch?v=5QUcaMavrSU.

Sommerová, Olga, dir. *Neznámí hrdinové – Pohnuté osudy*. "Krotitel esesáků – Fredy Hirsch." Aired 14 March 2011, on ČT2. Czech Republic, 2011.

Špaček, Radim, dir. *Člověk byl snadno vydíratelný*. Czech Republic: *Paměť Národa*, 2017.

Index

Note: Page numbers in *italics* indicate a figure.

abuse, 20, 33, 113; sexual, 20, 32–3, 45, 59, 74, 77–9, 120n101; verbal, 94–5, 96; victims, 78–9. *See also* sexual abuse of minors
Applebaum, Molly (Melania Weissenberg), 58, 89–96, *90*, *93*, *94*, *95*
Ashton, Bodie, 46
Aviram, Zvi (Heinz Abrahamsohn), 23, 26, 27–31

Backer, Sientje (née Stibbe), 13–15
Barnouw, David, 84, 88
Beachy, Robert, 57, 58
Beck, Gad, 7, *24*, *29*; and Aviram (Heinz Abrahamsohn), 26, 30–1; biography of, 22–4; and Dreyer, 32, 34; early life, 24–5, 31; in hiding and arrest of, 26; and Lewin, 25, 26–7; and Löwenstein, 23, 26, 27–8; move to Israel, 23; move to Palestine, 26; and Schwersenz, 25, 33–4; sister Miriam Rosenberg, 24, 25; *The Story of Gad Beck (Die Freiheit des Erzählens: Das Lebens des Gad Beck)* (documentary), 26–7, 30, 32; testimony of, 7, 9, 11; and Wählisch, 31–2. *See also* Chug Chaluzi, (The Circle of Pioneers)
Berlant, Lauren, 70
biological reductivism, 70
Bloomfield, Jacob, 46
Bondy, Ruth, 37
Breder, Linda (Reichová, Libuše), 15–18, *17*
Brom, Dotan, 44
Butler, Judith, 70

censorship, xvii, 37, 84, 86–8. *See also* queer Holocaust history
Centropa, 111–12. *See also* Serotta, Edward

Chug Chaluzi (The Circle of
  Pioneers), 25–6, 30, 35, 44
coercion, 77
crossdressing, 46–7. *See also* drag;
  female impersonators; Hambo;
  trans history

Dawidowicz, Lucy, 20–1
decriminalization of
  homosexuality, 8, 11, 55, 115n4
dependency, 57, 78
deviant, 2, 3, 13, 19, 21; depiction,
  36, 45, 118n52; "Hambo, the
  Pop-Hit Singer" (Lichtblau), 49
diaries. *See* Applebaum, Molly
  (Melania Weissenberg); Frank,
  Anne; Oppenhejm, Ralph;
  Redlich, Egon (Gonda)
disgust, 8, 39, 43
Doan, Laura, 58, 112
Does, Carsten, *29*
domestic abuse, 94–5
drag, 46, 49. *See also* female
  impersonators
Dwork, Debórah, 77

Ellenzweig, Allen, 82
enforced relationship, 113; queer
  relationship, 5
epistemic violence, 51
Eschebach, Insa, 8, 15
Evans, Jennifer, 3–4, 57–8
exploitation, 4, 57, 113
exploitative relationship. *See*
  relationship: exploitative;
  sexual violence

Fall, Susanne, 39
female impersonators, 46–7.
  See also drag; Hambo (Harry
  Heymann); trans history
female partner, 40. *See also*
  lesbian; queer women

female perpetrators, 22
Frank, Anne, 79–89; *The Betrayal
  of Anne Frank* (Sullivan),
  79–80; censorship of diary,
  83, 84, 86–8; *Diary of Anne
  Frank* (graphic novel) (Folman
  and Polonsky), 84–7, *85*, 88;
  gay uncles of, 83; queerness
  of, 80–6, *81*, 88–9. *See also*
  Maarsen, Jacqueline van
Frank, Otto, 84

gay: biographies/memoirs, 23,
  57–8; Chug Chaluzi, 35; Gad
  Beck, 22–3, 25, 27, 35; *Gay
  Berlin* (Beachy), 57; Frank
  Heibert, 23; Fredy Hirsch,
  43, 100; friendship, 121n119;
  Holocaust survivors, 2; Jiří
  Vrba, 97, 99, 104–12, 113;
  persecution against, 5–7, 10–12,
  21, 45; Ralph Oppenhejm, 38;
  rights movement, 8. *See also*
  homophobia; homosexuality
Geltungsjuden, 24–5, 26
gender non-conforming people,
  46. *See also* Hambo (Harry
  Heymann); trans history
Głowacka, Dorota, 79
Goldman, Sabina, 90–3, *93*, *94*,
  95–6
gossip, 17–18, 44, 48, 58, 83

Hambo (Harry Heymann), 45–50,
  52
"Hambo, the Pop-Hit Singer"
  (Lichtblau), *48*, 49
Hann, Cheryl, 80, 82, 84, 113
Heibert, Frank, 23, 28
Heinz Abrahamsohn (Zvi
  Aviram). *See* Aviram, Zvi
  (Heinz Abrahamsohn)
Helm, Sarah, 21–2

Herrn, Rainer, 46
Heuman, Margot, *61*, *67*, *69*; *The Amazing Life of Margot Heuman*, 70; awareness of sexual identity, 58, 60, 65, 67; and Hájková, 69; Holocaust archive interviews, 67–8; marriage and children, 66–7; and opera, 63; parents, 60–1, 64; queer kinship of, 57, 59, 72–3. *See also* Neumann, Edith (Dita)
Hirsch, Fredy, 36, 37, 40–1, *41*, 42, 43, 44–5, 52, 100, 102
homophobia: and an archaeological approach to history, 51–2; connection to dismissal from employment in Theresienstadt, 36–7; and decriminalization of homosexuality, 3, 7–8, 55; in description of Hambo, 49; and the gay rights movement in interwar Europe, 8; need for historicizing, 7–8; and portrayals of homosexuals, 1, 20–1; and queer kinship, 110; in survivor interviews, 2, 7–9, 10–13, 14–15, 68; in testimonies of survivors, 10–11; in historiography, 12–22. *See also* homosexuality; queerness
homosexuality: decriminalization of, 3, 8, 11, 55; pink triangle as signifier of, 5, 19, 32, 122n144; as prosecutable offense, 106, 108; and self-identification as gay, 35. *See also* gay; homophobia
Horowitz, Sara, 96

identity, 51, 111; intersectional, 45, 99; marker, 46. *See also* sexual identity; queerness

inclusive history, 22, 114
indexing, 10–13, *117*
intersectionality, 2, 107

Jensen, Edith, 50. *See also* Hambo
Jewish girls, 16, 17
Jones, William, 74, 76

kapos: abuse of pipel, 19, 20; Janek, 74–7, 78; as keyword, 11; as lesbians, 16, 18, 19. *See also* pipels
kinship, 57, 94, 113–14; Nate Leipciger and kapo, 78; queer (*see* queer kinship); units, 71–2, 73
Kohlmann, Anneliese, 65
Kosmala, Beate, 31
Kraus, Ota, 19, 22
Kulka, Erich, 19, 22

Langbein, Hermann, 20, 22
Langer, Lawrence, 57
Lapin, Andrew, 87, 88
Leipciger, Nate, *75*; fear of pregnancy, 75–6, 78; on loss of status as favorite, 77; sexual abuse of, 58, 59, 74–5, 78–9, 113; *The Weight of Freedom*, 79
Lenkawitzová, Anka, 61–2
lesbian desire: Applebaum's "lesbian love," 91; *The Well of Loneliness* (Hall), 54–5, *56*
lesbians: censorship of, 37; dismissals from employment in Theresienstadt, 36–8, 52; kapos as, 16, 18, 19; prisoners, 14–16, *17*; survivor, 59; in testimonies, 14–16; testimonies of, 59; working as guards, 21–2, 65–6. *See also* queer women
Lewin, Manfred, 26–7

Löwenstein, Oskar, 23, 26, 27–8
Lustig, Arnošt, 48–9

marginalization, 3, 53, 55
Marhoefer, Laurie, 38, 46
Mautner, Jan, 43–4
Melania Weissenberg. *See* Applebaum, Molly
Miller, Irene, 12
Milton, Sibyl, 71
Mischlinge, 24, 25. *See also Geltungsjuden*
mixed-sex camp, 36
molestation. *See* sexual abuse of minors
monosexual, 6, 36

Nestle, Joan: *The Well of Loneliness* (Hall), 54–5, 56
Neumann, Edith (Dita), 62, 63, 64–5, 66, 67, 68, 72–3
non-biological families, 59, 71–2, 114. *See also* queer kinship
norm, 3, 13, 21, 46, 52–3, 58, 83; biological families, 71, 114; queer kinship, 65, 72; teenage life, 66; sexuality, 55–6

Oppenhejm, Ralph, 38, 47–8
oral history, 11, 13, 98, 117n42, 119n85; interviews, 10, 23, 67–8, 108. *See also* oral history
othering, 8, 18, 21, 22, 49
outing, 7, 16, 27–8, 88

Pawełczynska, Anna, 21
pedophilia. *See* sexual abuse of minors
pipels, 6, 19, 20, 74. *See also* kapos; Leipciger, Nate
physical intimacy, 6, 27–34, 39, 47, 62, 78, 90, 100, 103
pink triangle, 19, 32, 122n144

Połtawska, Wanda, 21, 22
Povondra, Miloš, 107
power hierarchies, 3–4
prejudice, 1, 3, 9, 13, 22, 55
prisoner society, 4, 8, 22, 40, 55
prostitutes, 20; queer male prostitution, 48. *See also* sex work

queer biographies, 9, 12–13, 23, 46, 52, 59, 106
queer desire: attraction to minors, 44, 48–9; and the Frank family, 83; "getting hit on," 16, 18; in *People in Auschwitz* (Langbein), 20; silencing of, 113; understood as pedophilia, 20; viewed with disgust, 39. *See also individuals*; queer women
queer experience, 4–6, 21, 27, 97, 103; erasure of, 1, 10
queer Holocaust history: Belinfante, 10; choiceless choices, 57; and epistemic violence, 51; epistemology of the closet, 103; erasure of, 12, 37, 51–2, 68, 95, 113; Guttman, 9–10; historical citizenship, 50–1; intersectionality of, 2; Jews categorized as heterosexual, 2, 17–18; lack of research about, 2–3, 52–3; lack of testimonies in, 9–13, 51, 68; *People in Auschwitz* (Langbein), 19–20; research about, 6; Rosenstein, 9–10. *See also* Beck, Gad; censorship; pipels
queer kinship: and decision-making, 57, 113–14; as emancipatory, 110; versus family members, 59, 93–4, 96; practice of, 70–3. *See also*

relationships; same-sex
relationships
queer women: depiction in
camps, 8; lack of testimonials,
10. *See also* lesbians; queer
desire
queerness: 6–7, 27–8, 35, 58, 62–3,
82–3, 112. *See also* identity;
sexual identity

rape. *See* sexual violence
Rautenberg, Uta, 8
Rautenberg, Viola, 30
Redlich, Egon (Gonda), 36–7, 42
relationships, 12, 27–8, 30–1,
33–4, 37, 60, 114, 123n19;
and Anne Frank, 80, 82, 88;
emotional, 21; exploitative, 20;
family, 57; improper, 28; and
Nate Leipciger, 74, 76–8, 113;
with prisoner, 21; romantic,
4, 26, 30, 35, 65, 68–72, 100;
with teenagers, 32, 77; violent,
4–5, 78. *See also* abuse; queer
kinship; same-sex relationships
Ringelblum, Emanuel, 51
Rosenberg, Miriam (Miriam
Beck), 23

same-sex relationships, 3, 59,
73–4, 76–8; and attraction, 6–7;
censorship, 37; and experience,
1, 9; and intimacy, 6–7, 9.
See also individuals; queer
desire; queer kinship; sexual
identity; sexual intimacy
Schikorra, Christa, 12
Schwalb, Nathan, 26
Schwalbová, Manci, 16–18
Schwersenz, Jizchak, 23;
attraction to minors, 32–3,
44–5; and Beck, 25, 27–8,
32–3; and Chones, 25, 33;

lack of queer experiences in
testimony, 27; and Wolff, 25
secret police, 97, 106–8, 110–11,
127n117, 129n159
Serotta, Edward, 109, 111–12.
See also Centropa
sexual abuse of minors: in
Applebaum's diary, 90;
concealment of, in scholarship
on gay men in Nazi Germany,
45; connection to food, 74,
76; and consent, 77–8; and
German youth movement, 45;
of Leipciger, 74–5; of pipels,
19, 20, 74; queer desire as,
20; residential schools, 78–9;
Schwersenz's relationship with
teenagers, 32–3. *See also* Beck,
Gad
sexual barter: Beck's engagement
with, 26, 34; and coercion, 4, 34;
Hambo, 47–8; and kinship, 72;
Leipciger's engagement in, 58,
76, 77–8, 79; to save people, 34
sexual exploitation, 31–2, 113.
See also sexual violence
sexual identity: coming out,
60, 67, 110; Jews categorized
as heterosexual, 2, 17–18;
and marriage, 73; practice of
outing others, 7, 16–17, 27;
and same-sex intimacy, 7, 11.
See also Aviram, Zvi (Heinz
Abrahamsohn); Löwenstein,
Oskar; Vrba, Jiří
sexual intimacy: lack of
heterosexual opportunities
in camps, 36; relationship to
sexual identity, 7, 11; seeking
heterosexual intimacy after
camps, 58, 78
sexual violence: accidentally
implied in interviews, 18; in

sexual violence (*continued*)
  Beck's memoir, 31; and Dreyer, 32; rape, 34, 75, 76, 77, 120n101; towards Leipciger, 58, 59, 74–5, 78–9, 113
sex work, 47–8, 83. *See also* sexual barter
situational homosexuality, 21
Šmok, Martin, 109
Spivak, Gayatri, 51
Spořitel, Miroslav (pseudonym), 103, 105–6, 109
Stephens, Elizabeth, 8
stigma, 1–2, 21, 22
Stryker, Susan, 46

teenage prisoners, 19, 118n57
Terezín Initiative, 99, 108
testimonies: Beck's, 7, 9, 11; epistemology of the closet, 103; importance of, 50–1; of lesbians, 59; lesbians in, 14–16; no one discussed queerness at Centropa, 111–12; transgressive sexualities missing from queer Holocaust history, 9–13, 27–8, 51, 68, 97–8, 112; and Vrba, 97, 103, 104. *See also* oral history
Theresienstadt: children in, 61–2, 71, 102; Communist Party in, 101–2, 106; ethnicity as defining category in, 45; Family Camp, 42–3, 63–4, 102–3; Hambo in, 47; Mosse, 40; performances in, 63, 101, 108; social elite at, 39–40; Vrba's role in, 99
trans people, 5, 46–7, 116n21
trans history, 7, 46–7, 122n147

United States Holocaust Memorial Museum (USHMM), 23, 68, 95
unworthy victims, 20, 53

van Dijk, Lutz, 33
van Maarsen, Jacqueline, 80–1, 82, 86, 88–9
victim society, 46, 51–2, 72
victim-centred history, 5
Visual History Archive (VHA): lack of testimonies including transgressive sexualities, 10–13, *12*, 97–8; missing queerness, 68
Voigt, Martina, 27, 32
von der Heydt, Maria von der, 24
Vrba, Jiří, *98*, *101*, *109*; Communist Youth Union, 105; death, 109–10; deportation of, 63; early life, 99–100; family, 99–100, 102, 103, 104, 106, 109–10; first queer experience, 103; informant of Czechoslovakian secret state police, 97, 106–7, 108; and Kominíková, 100–1; lack of testimony from, 97, 103; living as self-identified gay man, 58–9, 97, 98, 104, 106, 110; Šling (cousin), 102, 105, 108; supporter of Communism, 107; and the theatre, 101, 105, 108; in Theresienstadt, 99, 100, 102–3; and Zuzana (niece), 105–6. *See also* Spořitel, Miroslav

Weissenberg, Melania. *See* Applebaum, Molly (Melania Weissenberg)
Weston, Kate, 70
women guards, 65. *See also* lesbians: working as guards
Wünschmann, Kim, 5

yizkor bikher, 50
young partners, 5